revelation driven prayer

DISCOVER THE SHOCK & AWE OF GOD'S VOICE

From the author of The Coming Church

JOHN BURTON

ISBN-13:
978-1463598587

ISBN-10:
1463598580

Published by Significant Publishing

Printed in the United States of America

To Amy, God's wonderful and precious gift to me.

john burton

is a church planter, conference speaker and author with a mandate to see the fire of God's presence invade cities and nations. He planted Revolution Church in Manitou Springs, Colorado and Revival Church in Detroit, Michigan.

John's ministry style could be described as wildly passionate, engaging, humorous and loaded with the flow and power of the Holy Spirit.

The prevailing theme of the ministry God has given John revolves around the topic of encountering God. Where God is, things happen. In His presence, the place where He is, is the fullness of joy. As we discover the wonderful mystery of walking in the Spirit, praying always and making aggressive strides in faith, life becomes incredible!

It truly is an experience in the invisible realm. As we tangibly experience God through deep and active prayer, we are interacting *in the Spirit.* As we walk by faith and understand how amazing a Holy Spirit driven life is, being a Christian believer quickly becomes the greatest adventure on earth!

John is currently focused on teaching, consulting, writing and ministering to churches.

If you would like to invite John to speak at your church, conference, camp or other event, please visit johnburton.net.

CONTENTS

Preface   7

Chapter One: Uncommon Sense   11

Chapter Two: Common Sense Has A Place   19

Chapter Three: Err On The Side Of Faith   23

Chapter Four: Decision Dilemma   27

Chapter Five: Uncommon Sense Scale   31

Chapter Six: Opposition From Those Who 'Know Better'   43

Chapter Seven: Fear Of Man In An Enemy Of Revelation   47

Chapter Eight: Steps Of A Righteous Man   53

Chapter Nine: God Said   61

Chapter Ten: Hearing Problems   69

Chapter Eleven: Revelation Driven Prayer   73

Chapter Twelve: We've Never Been This Way Before   91

Chapter Thirteen: A New Prayeradigm   95

Chapter Fourteen: Guard Against A Wondering Mind   105

PREFACE

Listen. Can you hear His voice? What's He saying?

Those questions have probably frustrated more people through the ages than we could fathom. Books have been written about unanswered prayer. The walls of pastor's and counselor's offices have soaked up countless quotes like, *"I don't hear God." "God doesn't talk to me." "I have no idea what I'm supposed to do."* And then, like clockwork, the question is asked to the counselor, *"What do YOU think I should do?"*

After all, to ask that question of someone we can see, and someone who can hear us, not to mention someone who will instantly talk back... audibly... so we can hear clearly and easily... seems to make a lot of sense. Certainly that person has the answers we're looking for, right? Well, sometimes yes, sometimes no.

In fact, if we are to fulfill our ministry, and if we are to move into uncharted territories, the majority of our direction will simply have to come directly from God himself. Others have not been where we are going!

> 1 Cor 2:5 ...your faith should not be in the wisdom of men but in the power of God.

If, throughout the Bible, God causes men and women to do things that defy human logic, why do we default to common sense when making decisions in our lives? If God told Gideon to secure only 1% of his army to go into battle, which obviously defies solid and time-tested military wisdom, why don't we consider that God may also cause us to advance in our lives via nontraditional and even bizarre means?

> Job 11:7 "Can you search out the deep things of God? Can you find out the limits of the Almighty?"

Deep things! The NIV calls them mysteries! God has an impossible job for us to accomplish, and it is going to take the Holy Spirit's creative ideas to fulfill our mission. If we cannot hear God, how can we confidently make decisions? On the contrary, if we do hear God, we will more certainly have the boldness and confidence to move ahead regardless of how foolish it may seem. We trust that God has more insight, revelation and wisdom than every other source of counsel available to us.

> Romans 11:33 Oh, the depth of the riches both of the wisdom and knowledge of God! How unsearchable are His judgments and His ways past finding out!

1 Cor 1:25 <u>Because the foolishness of God is wiser than</u>
<u>men, and the weakness of God is stronger than men.</u>

So, if we are operating in the instant, present Rhema wisdom of God, and that wisdom blows away the wisdom of man, that means many times *God will be calling us to do something very different than what common sense or human wisdom would suggest.* The advice in the counselor's office just won't cut it sometimes!

Is this to say we should never seek counsel? Of course not! The Bible states clearly that there is safety in a multitude of counselors. Absolutely! However, to *default to human logic in neglect of the present voice of God Himself is a very average, not to say dangerous way to live.*

CHAPTER ONE

UNCOMMON SENSE

Readers of this material will certainly come from a variety of backgrounds. For example, I would describe myself as a Charismatic Christian–someone who isn't impressed with artificial flamboyancy, but is quite impressed with the person and presence of the Holy Spirit as He manifests His presence. I often pray, *"Holy Spirit–come as You are and do what You want!"* Simply, if strange things happen, and God is in the midst of it, then great! If there is style with no substance, then it does little or no good. Other people come from backgrounds that cause them to be hesitant when it comes to the idea of hearing the ever-present voice of God. I was on a website today that discussed a large denomination's thoughts regarding the Rhema Word of God. They reject the idea that God is actively discussing things with us, as their belief is that the canon of Scripture is closed. They have adopted the cessationist position. There is no more talking to be done.

So, in order for this chapter, and this entire book to be understood, we have to embrace a common point of reference. We will come from the perspective that God, from a solid biblical base, is doing a lot of fresh and new things around the world, and much of it has been initiated by dreams, visions, prophecies or other supernatural insight. The key is that it cannot contradict Scripture. In fact, it will go very far in clarifying and supporting Scripture. The Logos will support the Rhema without exception.

The premise of this book is this—God is so deep, so powerful, so vast and so different than us, especially as people who live our lives in a 'suit of flesh', that *there simply must be more.* More to learn. More insight. Different perspectives. Powerful emotions. Clarifying revelation. Deep truths. The more we understand the depth of the character of God the easier it is to accept that supreme reliance on human common sense is actually detrimental to our Christian walk.

> *Eph 3:17-21 ...that you, being rooted and grounded in love, may be able to comprehend with all the saints what is the width and length and depth and height-- to know the love of Christ which passes knowledge; that you may be filled with all the fullness of God. Now to Him who is able to do exceedingly abundantly above all that we ask or think, according to the power that works in us, to Him be glory in the church by Christ Jesus to all generations, forever and ever. Amen.*

This passage declares that through faith *we can comprehend* the width and length and depth and height of the character of God. This is incredible! This passage also declares that God is able to do more than we can think or ask. So here we have an interesting paradox: in ourselves, we cannot humanly think up, ponder or create a common sense track for God to run on. He'll surprise us every time. Not only isn't the box big enough to contain Him, it's most certainly not the perfect shape, perfect depth or perfect volume. However, this passage also speaks to the idea that we can, through faith and through a wild and deep spiritual walk, comprehend and intimately know God.

How do we get from here to there? How do we experience this new wine of God? This new revelation of His desires? We must replace the old wine skins.

Where does knowledge come from? Past experience, either ours or another's. The same is true of human wisdom. We learn from what has already happened. The old wine skin can tell a lot. It has been affected by the wine. It has been conditioned by it. It smells like it. It is basically the perfect container for the old wine. They were made for each other. A match made in heaven!

However, there are some tragic missteps people take when relating to the old wineskin:

1. We learn to rely on what we can see. We can comprehend what has been done in the past. It makes sense. We can explain it, at least to a point. We can report on it. We can write about it. The danger? We become confident in what is seen instead of what is invisible. We walk by sight and not by faith.

2. We attempt to duplicate what has already been done. Or, we use what has been done as a comfortable foundation to add on to. The new wine, or the new plans of God cannot be contained in old containers. Old containers will resist the new substance it is being caused to contain. Remember, it's been conditioned by the old wine. It's not designed for something new.

Matt 9:16-17 "No one puts a piece of unshrunk cloth on an old garment; for the patch pulls away from the garment, and the tear is made worse. "Nor do they put new wine into old wineskins, or else the wineskins break, the wine is spilled, and the wineskins are ruined. But they put new wine into new wineskins, and both are preserved."

3. We become secure in the approval of man instead of the direction of God. There is a difference between *gaining wisdom* from man and *gaining approval* from man. Often we see what has already been done, and we like it. We can launch out in a new venture, a church growth method or a personal growth track that has already been 'proven' by another. This person may have written a book that has a lot of great insight. It may be a journal of what worked for them. It's an outline, for them, of new wine in a new wine skin. Here's a critical point–*For those who subscribe to another's method, it becomes an old wineskin that cannot contain the new wine God will be offering to us.* There is a place of perceived safety here as we can gain the approval of others as we move ahead in proven schemes for life. However, we neglect the Rhema, the new wine, if we refuse to take a risk, to enjoy godly wisdom while finding human approval unnecessary. The only way to discover a new wineskin is directly from God himself.

4. We limit the outcomes of our strategies to what has already been done. If we have a blue print of the Sears Tower in Chicago, and we put all of our resources into following those blueprints, what will we end up with? Another tower that looks just like the Sears Tower. How strange it would be to see a replica of that building in downtown Denver! Not only would it look silly, it would be a monument to foolishness. To use millions of dollars, thousands upon thousands of man hours and an extreme amount of energy over many years to produce a replica

of another man's creation is a terrible waste of God's creative resources.

Now, before I continue let me state something here. There is a place for common sense. This will be discussed further in another chapter, but for now let me say that there are truths that simply can't be violated. Many of these truths are scriptural truths. Others are plain old common sense. There are tried and true architectural guidelines that must be followed. A door, for example, should not be hung sideways.

The key here is that even with solid truths that cannot ever be violated, we can allow the new, fresh dreams of God to become reality. I would venture to say that every building in the world hangs doors up and down. However there are countless different types of doors and buildings. New innovations are continually being created.

Another way to say it is this: Imagine a roller coaster. The track represents the truth that must be held tightly to. The coaster represents us and our life, our journey. If we don't stay connected to the track, we will experience disaster! Just play one of those roller coaster simulations games on your computer for a bit and create a roller coaster that is designed in such a way that causes the coaster to fly off the track. It's a sight to behold! In the real world it's not a laughing matter.

However, the track, which represents the truth, is designed to take us places. So many people sit in their roller coaster firmly connected to the track–without going anywhere at all! Can you imagine how frustrating it would be for the next person in line if the coaster just sat there? We can trust the climbs and sharp turns and deep plunges that God has designed for us. There's a new thrill every ten feet if we only trust God to move! There's something new for us to experience!

Here's a personal insight—it's much better to seek the face of God for a brand new wine skin, an new container, a new and larger box AND enjoy a taste of *old wine* than to take someone's old *wine skin* for our own use. If the skin is old, we cannot put new wine into it. We miss out on God's directives for our current season of life. We can become frustrated as the old wine alone doesn't meet current needs. However, if we seek after a brand new design, a plan that has never been dreamed up, we can enjoy some powerful new wine while also respecting wine of old.

> Josh 3:3-4 "When you see the ark of the covenant of the LORD your God, and the priests, the Levites, bearing it, then you shall set out from your place and go after it. "Yet there shall be a space between you and it, about two thousand cubits by measure. Do not come near it, that you may know the way by which you must go, for you have not passed this way before."

We need a container of the Spirit of God that will take us places we've never gone. This is a critical point as God has big dreams for all of us. We cannot simply duplicate what has been done, because, well, we've been that way before! If the Spirit of God is moving one direction, we cannot become comfortable with another direction.

The Israelites became lovers of old wineskins. They desired Egypt even after liberation. The new wine of the Promised Land became undesirable because it would cause their skins, their faith, their flesh, everything about them to change radically. The old wineskins couldn't contain the new wine of victory in the Promised Land. The old wineskins couldn't contain the formula to even consider approaching the giants in the land. The strategies necessary to defeat these giants would only be contained in a brand new container. God was ready to transform the Israelites to the point were they would experience massive victory. But, it didn't work out that way. The only two wineskins that had been prepared for change were Joshua and Caleb. God had to basically eliminate all of the old wine skins and start with a fresh generation of people who were ready to move! Joshua, Caleb and the new generation were full of faith, obedience and the Spirit of God. They were prepared for the new wine, the new land and the big dreams of God.

When God told them to watch the Ark of the Covenant and follow it into a life of adventure He knew they were ready for some new wine, new victories and new miracles that would be talked about for centuries to come!

CHAPTER TWO

COMMON SENSE HAS A PLACE

As we gain understanding into the idea that God's plans often include something new and out of the ordinary, let's introduce some balance. It's very important to pursue the fresh ideas and dreams of God as God intends them to be pursued. Simply, we cannot invent or dream up some exciting and crazy idea in the attempt to facilitate something new. It must come from God himself. So, if we are prepared for the new wine and new directives of God, yet don't have the instructions or vision, we must proceed with wisdom and common sense.

Consider the blueprints for the building. The possibilities are limitless as we let God reveal His perfect creative drawings to us. Anything from the next Sears Tower to another Superdome to something never even contemplated in the minds of man is possible. We can dream big! But, unless the designer gives directives for some radical new idea for a door, there are only a handful of options available to us. Common sense would be correct in telling us that the door must swing open. It must have some sort of handle or way to open it. In certain situations, it should have a locking mechanism. While God can do anything He desires, including creating the next 'dream door', unless we have those designs, we can use the 'brain God gave us' and make the best decision possible.

If we feel impressed that we are to become a dentist, and we know God has big plans for us as a dentist, we must still exercise common sense and wisdom in the process. Faith may be required to gain the financing to be able to attend college. Common sense tells us in order to become a dentist we must attend college. Faith may give us supernatural ability to market ourselves and open the best dentist's office in the city. Common sense tells us that we must have business hours and schedule appointments if we are to make money.

I know this sounds overly simplistic, but all too often we can either over or under spiritualize things. On one hand we may have little faith and lean heavily on what has worked in the past. This, as has been discussed, can cause us to live discouraging lives. On the other hand, we can launch out in tangents of supposed faith that God never intended us to go in. That's why it is so important that we discover the art of hearing God. His voice is the critical piece of the puzzle that will cause us to know how to move, both spiritually and practically.

To rely on common sense or human wisdom without the voice of God continually echoing in our spirits can cause great catastrophe.

> *Ezek 28:3-5 (Behold, you are wiser than Daniel! There is no secret that can be hidden from you! With your wisdom and your understanding You have gained riches for yourself, And gathered gold and silver into your treasuries; By your great wisdom in trade you have increased your riches, And your heart is lifted up because of your riches)*

However, the Word also declares that wisdom and understanding can help us greatly in life if we use them correctly.

> *Prov 3:13 Happy is the man who finds wisdom, And the man who gains understanding;*

The Proverbs are full of verses of common sense, one after another. Now, of course, Proverbs is a part of the living Word of God. We can't accurately proclaim that the proverbs are simply common sense since they were breathed from the mouth of God. However, they are indicative of usually simple and often practical truths that simply can't be compromised.

What's the bottom line? Listen to God. When you don't hear Him, do what your situation calls for. Gain insight from others, the Bible and your own wisdom. Don't be afraid to step out. As we'll discuss later, the Word declares that the steps of a righteous man are ordered of God. We can be confident in moving forward if we are righteous, separated to and intimate with God. He'll take good care of us whether we're moving in bold faith steps or even in steps of wisdom and common sense.

CHAPTER THREE

ERR ON THE SIDE OF FAITH

As New Testament believers, it seems as if we should live our lives by a different code and in a different dimension. The rules are different here. If this is the case, why do we so quickly look for practical and logical solutions to life's problems and goals?

Even in the church planting world, the most common discussions on how to be successful revolve around structures, theories, success stories and effective programs. Of course, such discussion can be educational and helpful, though I'm concerned at the overwhelming lack of balance. Where are the discussions on faith? Are people still discussing the power of prayer?

Throughout the Bible, as has been stated, story after story, principle after principle, truth after truth perpetuates the idea of stepping out into the impossible. Peter did it on the water. Moses did it at the Red Sea. Gideon did it with the Mideonites. David did it with Goliath. The stories are seemingly endless.

If this is the case, why do we so often choose to err on the side of safety? On the side of practicality? On the side of logic? The Bible clearly directs us to lean NOT on our own understanding. I don't know how many times I've made a step of faith that caused eyebrows to raise. I would hear things like, *"That doesn't make sense."* Or, *"You need to do what has been successful in the past."* Or, *"Where did you come up with that crazy idea?"* Or very often, *"You really should gain a consensus, wait it out, don't rush to a decision."*

Now, in certain instances some of those suggestions would certainly be valid. As has been stated, there is a very important place for Godly wisdom. However, the closer we get to God, the clearer His voice becomes, and the more urgent a decisive response becomes, the more confident we can be in making some radical decisions. In this situation, as we are clearly hearing God's voice, it becomes critical that we err on the side of faith rather than safety. Too many times, human logic has caused one to ignore a directive from Heaven.

An age old question we can ask ourselves is, *"What do I have to lose?"*

If the answer has to do with the loss of respect, loss of friends, loss of safety, loss of comfort, etc., then the answer should be easy. Simply listen to God, capture His heart, and leap in faith! Really, this is an obedience issue. If we choose to err on the side of safety, or the side of maintaining a reputation, then we very possibly may be disobeying God. To be a New Testament believer requires us to live a miraculous life just to be obedient! A New Testament life is an impossible life. So, it only makes 'sense' to expect that most of our key decisions in life will require faith to be successful. We should expect faith to be required. To avoid situations that require faith truly may require disobedience!

The Bible makes it very clear that, when confronted with a difficult decision, or any decision for that matter, that we are to make a step of faith as opposed to one guided by sight. What we see is not as real as what we cannot see.

> *2 Corinthians 5:7 For we walk by faith, not by sight.*

> *Matthew 8:26 But He said to them, "Why are you fearful, O you of little faith?" Then He arose and rebuked the winds and the sea, and there was a great calm.*

I can hear the arguments now, *"Well, you should only make such a faith step that defies age old wisdom if you know that you know that you know that God has told you something. Otherwise, you should side with wisdom."*

I agree! This is an interesting point. It may seem as if I'm supporting a haphazard lifestyle. I am not in anyway. Foolishness is not an option. If we are not hearing God clearly, then we must gain some solid wisdom from some pillars of the church. Of course, the Word of God is always the final authority.

But, the argument that is being made is really not against the seeking of counsel. What is most often heard is a subtle chuckle and smirk when the idea of hearing God is raised. Most people don't truly believe that God speaks clearly and continually to those who are listening! Since they have learned to make their own way, and since they don't subscribe to the idea that God is in constant communication with His people, they believe those who make radical steps of crazy faith to be foolish.

> *Mark 5:35-36 While He was still speaking, some came from the ruler of the synagogue's house who said, "Your daughter is dead. Why trouble the Teacher any further?"*

As soon as Jesus heard the word that was spoken, He said to the ruler of the synagogue, "Do not be afraid; only believe."

The unbelievers in the crowd (note they called Jesus 'Teacher', they were in the 'church crowd') were highlighting the obvious–the girl was dead. They were saying, *"Give us a break! It's a done deal. She is gone."* However, faith prevailed. Jesus instructed the man to take a faith step- to fear not and to believe. This step resulted in a miracle.

Whatever you do, don't let fear of man stop you from being confident in your relationship with Jesus! The Holy Spirit is active and God is speaking. He will give impossible and radical directives to those who are willing to listen and obey. If we desire to be average Christians, we can err on the side of logic and safety. But, those who wish to venture into a different dimension, into a place of miracles, risk and big dreams then, every day, listen to God, hear Him share his His dreams and err continually on the side of faith.

CHAPTER FOUR

DECISION DILEMMA

So, what's your heart telling you? What was your first inclination? We've all heard advice like this when attempting to make a decision. While advice like that is not as full grown and mature as it should be, it's really closer to solid advice for the Spirit-driven believer than one might suppose. When it comes time to make a decision, so many people get stuck in a holding pattern. Most every week people come to me with the question, *"What do you think I should do?"* The fear in decision making is often very extreme, and for believers, that fear is often rooted in doubt. Doubt that God will bless their decision. Doubt that they will do what God wants them to do. Doubt that there is any grace at all if they make a mistake!

> *Prov 3:5-7 Trust in the LORD with all your heart, And lean not on your own understanding; In all your ways*

acknowledge Him, And He shall direct your paths. Do not be wise in your own eyes;

This is an intriguing verse. Note that it doesn't say, *"Trust in the Lord and if things don't make sense, don't freak out, but relax and everything will soon make sense."*

If that were a verse, it would certainly be found in the Message version! But, of course it is not. The verse actually tells us to basically resist our own understanding. To put little confidence in it. When I find myself saying, "I just don't understand," I get excited! This verse is a perfect verse for this book. It's the epitome of uncommon sense. Our own understanding, whether making decisions or developing strategies, can lead us astray. It can lead us into the predictable. It can be boring!

If we tend to make decisions based upon human wisdom, on proven strategies, then we limit God in ways beyond explanation. In essence, when we add prayer to that mind-set, *we are asking God to bless our common plans instead of being available to bless God's uncommon plans!*

The key to making uncommon sense decisions is our prayer life. If we are praying continually, without ceasing, then we will hear God easily. We will capture His heart. We will know His desires. The sheep hear His voice.

> *John 10:3-4 To him the doorkeeper opens, and the sheep hear his voice; and he calls his own sheep by name and leads them out. And when he brings out his own sheep, he goes before them; and the sheep follow him, for they know his voice.*

Amy and I were house shopping in Manitou Springs a few years ago. We looked at several homes, and a few seemed like good possibilities. We spent a lot of time and energy figuring out how to get into these homes. One by one they fell through. Then, a few weeks later, our realtor took us into a home that was right across the street from the church. The split second Amy and I walked through the door, we knew we were to buy that house. We walked through it and then told our realtor to write up the contract. He was surprised. Didn't we want to do some homework? Certainly we should pray about it, right? That's the normal course of action. However, as we were already praying without ceasing, additional prayer was not necessary. We had our answer.

It didn't make common sense to proceed that way, but this decision was made as the Spirit led. The selling price of the house was exactly what we were pre-approved for. However, we discovered that the closing costs would take us beyond that limit. The limit was firm. The seller of the house wouldn't drop the price of the house, nor would he cover any closing costs. The door seemed closed. However, Amy and I didn't even pray about it again! We knew the house was ours. We waited less than a day, and the realtor called us back. He said the owner agreed to cover 1/2 of the closing costs, AND our realtor and the seller's realtor agreed to cover the remaining costs out of their commission!

That decision that was made in an instant resulted in a perfectly happy ending because we didn't lean on our own understanding. We were praying without ceasing. We knew in our spirit what God wanted for us. The roadblocks didn't even phase us. The testimony of that story has encouraged many people in our church. That kind of story can happen to each of us as we rely first on the uncommon sense of the Spirit of God. As we lean not on our own understanding. As the obvious is ignored as we respond to a supernatural directive of God.

All throughout Scripture we encounter decisions that defy human wisdom. David refused to wear the appropriate armor. Gideon took 1% of his potential army with him. Jesus put mud in somebody's eyes. In fact, the uncommon surpasses the common with incredible regularity.

If we can pay the price to continually pray, we'll continually hear God's voice. As we dive deeper into our discussion of *Revelation Driven Prayer*, we'll see that living a life like that requires hearing God's voice. As we do, our life will become radically different as we make decisions that defy human logic, that cause eyebrows to raise, and that will result in miraculous ending after miraculous ending!

> *Job 37:5 God thunders marvelously with His voice; He does great things which we cannot comprehend.*

CHAPTER FIVE

UNCOMMON SENSE SCALE

We all start our Christian lives from a logical and emotional standpoint. At this early stage, we are very in tune with logical trains of thought and with our emotions and desires. Our spirits are yet to be nurtured. That's the very idea of being born again. It's a new start.

However, to continue our lives as believers driven by logic and emotion is a tragic mistake. Logic and emotions rely on fact, or at least natural perception. They are driven by what can be seen, examined and understood. While emotions can certainly be illogical, they are so strong at times that we rely on the translation of data they provide as opposed to walking in faith.

A new believer logically arrives at the conclusion that they don't have what it takes to get to heaven. They can't even succeed on this planet. They realize they need a Savior. They are at a place of personal

BURTON UNCOMMON SENSE SCALE

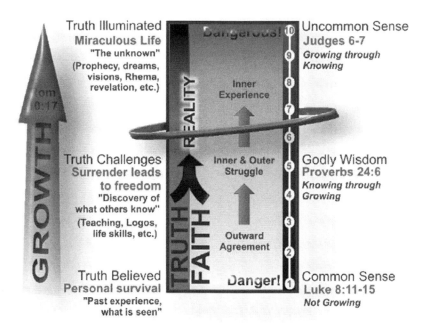

survival. Their past experiences and what they can quantify in their own lives add up to failure. This fact results in the surrender of their life.

If you look at the scale, you will notice two bars–a dark one and a lighter one. The dark bar represents truth. You will see that this bar remains constant from bottom to top. The only change is at the top, which represents a life of extreme *uncommon sense*, that truth is so active and alive that it darkens to black.

In contrast, the lighter bar, which represents faith, starts very dim at the bottom and gradually darkens upward. At the bottom, faith absolutely exists. Nobody can find God without faith. Basic biblical truth is agreed with and basic faith is present. The radical miracle is that this is all it takes to become a follower of Jesus Christ! God understands our limitations!

However, to remain at this logical and emotive stage is terribly dangerous. In all reality, it simply cannot be done. Either grow into a person of extreme and blind faith, or fall away. Period.

Let's read a passage of Scripture that is familiar to all of us:

> *Luke 8:4-8 And when a great multitude had gathered, and they had come to Him from every city, He spoke by a parable: "A sower went out to sow his seed. And as he sowed, some fell by the wayside; and it was trampled down, and the birds of the air devoured it. Some fell on rock; and as soon as it sprang up, it withered away because it lacked moisture. And some fell among thorns, and the thorns sprang up with it and choked it. But others fell on good ground, sprang up, and yielded a crop a hundredfold." When He had said these things He cried, "He who has ears to hear, let him hear!"*

Jesus goes on to explain this parable:

> *Luke 8:11-15 "Now the parable is this: The seed is the word of God. Those by the wayside are the ones who hear; then the devil comes and takes away the word out of their hearts, lest they should believe and be saved. But the ones on the rock are those who, when they hear, receive the word with joy; and these have no root, who believe for a while and in time of temptation fall away. Now the ones that fell among thorns are those who, when they have heard, go out and are choked with cares, riches, and pleasures of life, and bring no fruit to maturity. But the ones that fell on the good ground are those who, having heard the word with a noble and good heart, keep it and bear fruit with patience."*

This is a very important story as it highlights the critical importance of continual growth. This is what the Uncommon Sense Scale is all about–living a life of faith, growth and fruit.

Jesus continues in Luke by saying,

Luke 8:17-18 "For nothing is secret that will not be revealed, nor anything hidden that will not be known and come to light. Therefore take heed how you hear. For whoever has, to him more will be given; and whoever does not have, even what he seems to have will be taken from him."

It's important that we continue to 'have stuff' from God! We must grow, receive from Him more and more maturity, focus, passion, increased faith and a determination to press on toward the goal.

Let's begin at the lowest point on the scale–the place of common sense. At this point, a person simply is drawn into a relationship with Jesus usually through a realization of their situation. Their eyes have been opened to the light of the Gospel. We all start right here.

The seed is planted in a brand new heart. As I stated previously, this is a very dangerous position to remain in. A seed must be planted, fertilized and watered to grow. It must be carefully nourished or it will die. On the right side of the scale, you will notice it is numbered beginning at the bottom from one to ten. We are at number one right now. There is more walking by sight than by faith at this stage. This must change if we are to move into a place of stability and growth.

Let me remind you the key to growth, the key to living a life of uncommon sense and revelation–we must HEAR God!

Romans 10:17 So then faith comes by hearing, and hearing by the word of God.

That's it! To grow, to venture into the impossible New Testament life that God has for all of us, we must be people of great faith.

To take steps of faith, we must hear God. He talks, we listen and we move.

Ok, back to the scale. This lower level is also a place of what I call *outward agreement*. Simply, we are driven primarily by our circumstances. What is going on in our world is the basis for our decision to follow Christ. It's the 'rock bottom' reality that so many people must experience before they admit they need Jesus. Some actually do hit rock bottom while others wise up at another point in the process and admit Jesus is the only answer. Regardless, the point here is that the dominant stream of data that causes us to react comes from circumstance. We 'agree' that life is tough and we want to discover how to 'beat it'. This is the place of pure survival. It's a crisis point.

The sad truth is that many believers don't progress past this point. The reality is that those who literally don't progress past this very elementary stage most often backslide rather quickly. The conquering of the issues of life simply aren't resolved at this stage. To discover the riches of the Word of God, that *Word must be heard* and heeded. We must grow. If we don't, we soon realize that 'getting saved' isn't a magic pill that we take to eliminate depression, fear, anxiety, doubt, hatred, lust and any number of other bondages people, both saved and unsaved, experience. No, we must grow to the next level and it's going to take faith to get us there.

People who enter stage one come to the point where they believe the truth. They believe Jesus is the Son of God, He died and rose again and He is their only hope. While stage one emphasizes many of the benefits of the Word of God, stage two is radically different. In stage one, truth is believed. In stage two, truth challenges. It's the place of inward and outward struggle. While it's impossible to have statistics on such a topic, I would guess greater than 80% of believers never progress beyond this stage. It's this stage where we are confronted with our weaknesses, our issues and our future. This future demands a radical confrontation with our own inner issues.

Most churches preach to people at this level, and to a degree this is appropriate. It's a place where we learn from other's experiences. Godly wisdom is transferred. Scriptural truth challenges us as it did the one who is teaching it. Books are read and we allow them to challenge us. We listen to sermons, watch Christian television and do our best to allow our spirits and minds to be rattled to the point of growth.

> Proverbs 24:6 For by wise counsel you will wage your own war, And in a multitude of counselors there is safety.

While the first stage is defined by the fact that we're really not growing all that much, the second stage is the opposite. It's defined by the fact that we are growing. We're *knowing through growing*, or we're allowing our faith to increase, we're discovering Holy Spirit communicated truths by intentionally seeking after teaching from others. It's a place of surrender of self as we're guided into truth through people by the Holy Spirit. We are discovering that there are some ways to live that don't compute to the natural mind. For example, common sense would tell us that giving away 10% of our income simply doesn't lead to financial independence. It literally results in a net loss. However, as we are allowing ourselves to be challenged by some seemingly nonsensical principles in the Word of God, tithing somehow now just makes sense. Our inner spirit man is responding to this food! We are surrendering our old way of thinking and allowing our minds to be renewed, allowing old things to pass away and the new things of God to take root in our lives.

Now it gets exciting! As we move up the scale to the third stage, truth and faith merge to reveal to us an amazing reality! Dreams, visions and a miraculous life emerge at this stage. Our decisions are made via the prompting of the ever present voice of the Holy Spirit as opposed to what just 'makes sense'. We are able to stand on the Word of God in ways that defy logic. Faith explodes here. It is the place of uncommon sense. As we'll see, living a revelation driven life requires that we step into this place of fresh faith.

In the second stage, we were 'knowing through growing'. Now, we are 'growing through knowing'. We are hearing fresh data from God, we are intimate with Him, we are dreaming dreams. The Word of God is exploding off the pages. Now, our experience with God is measured exponentially. Our knowing of God results in phenomenal and continual and rapid growth. It's at this place where the mighty men and women of God emerge.

This stage is epitomized in the story of Gideon in Judges 6 and 7. Nothing Gideon did made sense. However, he was able to fulfill his mission because he was able to hear God speak. Gideon went from a person of common sense to a person of uncommon sense overnight! Let's look at this story.

> *Judges 6:1-6 Then the children of Israel did evil in the sight of the Lord. So the Lord delivered them into the hand of Midian for seven years, and the hand of Midian prevailed against Israel. Because of the Midianites, the children of Israel made for themselves the dens, the caves, and the strongholds which are in the mountains. So it was, whenever Israel had sown, Midianites would come up; also Amalekites and the people of the East would come up against them. Then they would encamp against them and destroy the produce of the earth as far as Gaza, and leave no sustenance for Israel, neither sheep nor ox nor donkey. For they would come up with their livestock and their tents, coming in as numerous as locusts; both they and their camels were without number; and they would enter the land to destroy it. So Israel was greatly impoverished*

because of the Midianites, and the children of Israel cried out to the Lord.

Here we see stage one. It was a time of crisis. The evil Israelites were living a life of common sense. They simply knew they were under attack and they had to protect themselves. They did what made sense by preparing shelters in the caves. They had to figure out a way to protect their crops. They were in survival mode. So, what did they do? They did what every person who recognizes their need of a savior does–they cried out to God for help, for salvation.

> *Judges 6:7-10 And it came to pass, when the children of Israel cried out to the Lord because of the Midianites, that the Lord sent a prophet to the children of Israel, who said to them, "Thus says the Lord God of Israel: 'I brought you up from Egypt and brought you out of the house of bondage; and I delivered you out of the hand of the Egyptians and out of the hand of all who oppressed you, and drove them out before you and gave you their land. Also I said to you, "I am the Lord your God; do not fear the gods of the Amorites, in whose land you dwell." But you have not obeyed My voice.'*

God responded to them via a prophet who simply told them to obey God. It's the most basic call of relationship: obey God, love Him and let Him love you and take care of you.

> *Judges 6:11-12 Now the Angel of the Lord came and sat under the terebinth tree which was in Ophrah, which belonged to Joash the Abiezrite, while his son Gideon threshed wheat in the winepress, in order to hide it from the Midianites. And the Angel of the Lord appeared to him, and said to him, "The Lord is with you, you mighty man of valor!"*

Now Gideon is addressed as someone who is already at stage three–a mighty warrior. Of course, this truth confounded Gideon as all he could see is that his nation was being annihilated before his very eyes. He was, just like the rest of the Israelites, a survivalist.

> *Judges 6:13 Gideon said to Him, "O my lord, if the Lord is with us, why then has all this happened to us? And where are all His miracles which our fathers told us about, saying, 'Did not the Lord bring us up from Egypt?' But now the Lord has forsaken us and delivered us into the hands of the Midianites."*

Did I mention that complaining and blaming God most often occurs at stage one? After all, Christianity is a magic pill that makes everything better, right? Gideon revealed his immaturity by putting the blame for all of the tragedy he was experiencing right on God's shoulders. God seemingly had all of the responsibility and Gideon had none.

However, God is merciful and coaxes Gideon out of stage one and into stage two:

> *Judges 6:14 Then the Lord turned to him and said, "Go in this might of yours, and you shall save Israel from the hand of the Midianites. Have I not sent you?"*

God is placing the responsibility squarely on Gideon's shoulders. It's time to grow. It's time for a challenge.

> *Judges 6:15 So he said to Him, "O my Lord, how can I save Israel? Indeed my clan is the weakest in Manasseh, and I am the least in my father's house."*

Oh, the dance has begun! Gideon was now presented with an impossible mission and all he can resort to is his common sense. He's weak. His family is weak. He's obviously the wrong choice.

Judges 6:16 And the Lord said to him, "Surely I will be with you, and you shall defeat the Midianites as one man."

After this, Gideon was well into stage two. As the story unfolds, Gideon asks God for confirmation in a few different ways. The higher up the scale we go, the more mature we are, the less we will require God to confirm His Word!

We will hear Him and simply know that His promises are yes and amen! There is no more doubting, no more fear, no more wavering. God said it and we believe it! Gideon wasn't quite there yet.

Gideon was then directed to tear down his father's altar. This was a nonsensical directive to say the least! He wasn't only messing with his family, but with the entire camp. He never would have done this without hearing the voice of God. Remember, the issue at hand is protecting the crops and their lives from attack. This part of the equation didn't seem to fit, but Gideon was obedient. He was inching closer to stage three as a mighty man of God!

Now, after some further tests to ensure he was hearing God, Gideon grew into a man of uncommon sense and revelation driven prayer. He was hearing God's voice as it thundered louder than his own thoughts.

If Gideon were to sit down with the leaders and military experts in the camp's board room and take a vote on how to attack, there is no way he would have come out of there with a battle plan like he received directly from God. Remember, we cannot embrace a democratic mind-set when living a life of uncommon sense. It's true, many people will look at us and say, *"Nonsense!"* However, whom do we serve?

Gideon ended up telling 99% of the people that God didn't need them. Imagine the opportunity for offense to rise up from within some incredibly faithful people! The second guessing, the murmuring, the gossip, the opinions, the scrutiny! After all, he's the youngest of the weakest! Who is Gideon to tell me to go home! Who is he to tell me I'm not fit for battle! And, all because I got on my knees to take a drink of water? This absolutely makes no sense! You can't devise a plan of battle like this!

Now we're in the place of amazing faith! The story continues with a dream. We need a dream in our camp! The interpretation of this dream resulted in the advance against the Mideonites camp. Gideon was well into stage three as a mighty man of valor.

He now had the confidence to follow the instructions of the Lord. He had grown up overnight.

> *Judges 6:17-23 Then he said to Him, "If now I have found favor in Your sight, then show me a sign that it is You who talk with me. Do not depart from here, I pray, until I come to You and bring out my offering and set it before You." And He said, "I will wait until you come back." So Gideon went in and prepared a young goat, and unleavened bread from an ephah of flour. The meat he put in a basket, and he put the broth in a pot; and he brought them out to Him under the terebinth tree and presented them. The Angel of God said to him, "Take the meat and the unleavened bread and lay them on this rock, and pour out the broth." And he did so. Then the Angel of the Lord put out the end of the staff that was in His hand, and touched the meat and the unleavened bread; and fire rose out of the rock and consumed the meat and the unleavened bread. And the Angel of the Lord departed out of his sight. Now Gideon perceived that He was the Angel of the Lord. So Gideon said, "Alas, O Lord God! For I have seen the Angel of the*

Lord face to face." Then the Lord said to him, "Peace be with you; do not fear, you shall not die."

The battle was won! Why? Because someone had the guts to hear God and act regardless of what man might think or whether his own life would be lost. He simply heard God and obeyed. He was not a man who lived a life of nonsense, as some would say. He was simply a man of uncommon sense and he fulfilled his mission.

CHAPTER SIX

OPPOSITION FROM THOSE
WHO 'KNOW BETTER'

Ask ten people what they think some of the non-negotiable elements are for any particular growth strategy and you will get at least 5 different answers. You will also discover some experts, both actual and self-proclaimed, who will be adamant about how you must proceed. Some will have your best interest at heart while others are simply zealous about their past successes, their strategies and their insight. Be humble… and beware!

- *Be humble– God will use many different types of people to speak into your life.*
- *Beware– So will the devil.*

   If you are truly a person of uncommon sense, you will frustrate or even irritate many who just can't imagine why you can't see things their way. After all, the high majority would side with them! Plus, they have practical experience–their advice is the direct result of what has worked for them and possibly even countless others. They would say that it is a tried and true strategy.

The problem? That advice, that strategy that is so obviously effective and appropriate, may simply not be God's desired plan of action for you. It really is that simple, and we must consider that possibility at every turn of our lives.

This is a very difficult place for some people to navigate through. A Spirit-driven person with a unique directive from God will not always be able to intellectually explain why they are doing what they are doing. *People will believe you are nonsensical when in reality you are simply using a different set of senses.* Our intellect is taking a back seat to our spirit.

When people come to me with directives and wisdom that is contrary to what God has spoken to me, I will first consider their insight. I will pray about it–sometimes on the spot and sometimes over several days or even longer. If the time comes that I feel led to continue as I have felt the Lord has directed, I'll sometimes challenge the individual, especially if they persist.

I'll ask them to share their understanding of how they feel I should proceed. I'll then alert them to the Scripture that warns us about leaning on our own understanding. We simply cannot assume we know the course another individual should take at all times. We cannot always rely on common sense. In fact, as a believer, *MOST of what we do will defy common sense!* We should we wary of steps that have been repeated through the ages. We should expect something fresh and new!

A disclaimer: we must remember that things radically change when an authority in our lives addresses us. We must submit to them and honor them fully.

A great example of this came my way a few days ago. Revolution House of Prayer is unapologetically a burning ministry of intercession. We are a team of white hot believers who know we can move mountains more quickly with our mouth than with a pick and shovel. We are specialists with a focused mission. There is much that we will not do. There is much that we will do.

A man, who's heart was most probably innocent and broken for the lost, approached me and another pastor. His approach was far from appropriate, but let's look past that. He berated us for not advancing our ministries according to 'tried and true principles'.

"Are you going door to door? Why not? This pastor and that pastor did go door to door and look how their churches are growing. I want you to start going door to door now!"

He was effectively leaning on his own understanding. He witnessed a strategy work in other environments and he couldn't imagine why every pastor didn't do the same thing. He presumed everything from ignorance to rebellion to laziness were the reasons. It made no sense to him why one would focus on prayer and not on evangelism. It's probably because he's an evangelist at heart!

I told him that God has not released me to do any sort of organized outreach for the first 5 years of this ministry! He was shocked. I went on to explain our very unique vision and strategy. I don't know that I convinced him of anything, but that wasn't my goal. I didn't need his approval. I fear God and know that to take Manitou Springs for Jesus will take a far out vision. The first part of Acts chapter 2 must precede the second part. The power comes first, and then the mission.

Rumor has it that fourteen churches have started and failed in their first 2 years since the 1980's in Manitou Springs. Revolution has been healthy, strong and effectively advancing for nearly 6 years now. We're hearing God and He's blessing in powerful and fresh ways.

Some are to plant. Some are to water. Some are to prophesy, some teach, some evangelize, some pastor. We all receive a unique mix of gifts, dreams, visions and strategies. Don't attempt to fit into some mold. Don't copy what has already been done. Be a trailblazer and go where no man has gone before!

> Joshua 3:3,4 "When you see the ark of the covenant of the Lord your God, and the priests, the Levites, bearing it, then you shall set out from your place and go after it. Yet there shall be a space between you and it, about two thousand cubits by measure. Do not come near it, that you may know the way by which you must go, for you have not passed this way before."

Bottom line—if nobody has been this way before, *others won't have the key strategic components that you will need.* Only the presence of God will pave the way for you to know which way to go. Keep your eyes on God, not man and you'll do just fine.

Here's the question—do you have the humility to submit yourself to your authorities and the guts to press through the nay sayers toward the very personal goal that God has given you? Will you obey His call? Will you carry the responsibility that few may agree with or understand?

Just remember this—when things start to make sense in your intellect, take heed—don't lean on that understanding. Rather submit the issue to the Holy Spirit and expect some wild and crazy replies from a very creative God!

CHAPTER SEVEN

FEAR OF MAN IS AN ENEMY OF UNCOMMON SENSE & REVELATION DRIVEN PRAYER

An entire book could be written on this topic, and, in fact, many have been. Let's approach this from the perspective of a dreamer. To have a dream is deeply personal, unique and specialized for the person who has received it. A dreamer, or a visionary, who is spending countless hours in the presence of God and who is burning in their spirits to see their vision fulfilled has an important job to do–advance!

They are with God constantly and have heard His voice. The goal is clear. The stirring is endless. However, the process very well may not be clear, or at least it may not be easily communicable. Any visionary who has ever done anything worth writing home about has had to advance, to a large degree, alone. Why is this? The more impossible the dream, the more radical the approach must be. The more radical the approach is, the more it is scrutinized.

Few people ever understand what goes on inside prophetic people who see with spiritual eyes. Therefore, especially if they are in close relationship with the visionary, and ESPECIALLY if they are under the influence of their leadership, their lack of comfort in the process can easily result in a visible lack of support.

They certainly see point A. They see where you are, your weaknesses, your limits and your general situation in life. They may even be able to see point B. The goal may be a great one. There may be agreement on the value of it. It may even generate some excitement. The problem lies on that seemingly never ending dotted line between point A and point B. People who haven't directly received the vision may, out of frustration or even pride, be relentless in offering their two cents on how to fulfill the mission. To them it seems obvious. Maybe they have done it that way in the past. The problem is that they haven't been given the dream. It's not theirs.

To further muddy the waters, the visionary may truly not understand the process either. It's at this point that living a Spirit-led life becomes as critical as life and death itself. The visionary may be receiving a steady stream of ideas, concerns, opinions and pressure from well meaning, and sometimes not so well meaning, people. This type of situation seemingly highlights brightly the weakness and apparent lack of the visionary. The visionary doesn't know how to proceed and the critic has any number of great ideas to offer.

At this point the person who has been entrusted with the precious and sensitive dreams of God must be absolutely free from the fear of man. Fear of scrutiny, of weaknesses being exposed, of murmuring, of not knowing how to defend your position—it all must be broken in our lives. Remember Gideon's plight. He was called to obey God's instructions that were seemingly ridiculous. Of course, they were the only instructions that would work!

There are many times in our lives where we will receive counsel from well meaning people, and we'll know in our spirit that we are not to proceed in that direction. Of course, there are times where we seek out counsel from people that the Lord directs us to. There are experts out there who have both practical and spiritual insight that is important to grasp. However, whether we are seeking counsel or whether it's simply offered to us, we must hear the voice of God ourselves. Confirmation in our spirit is non-negotiable.

I'll share with people this perspective in such situations:

> *"I appreciate your ideas, but I want you to realize something. As convinced as you are that you are right, and that I must proceed as you feel directed, please understand that you would cause me to disobey what I believe God is telling me to do if I went in that direction. If your position is confirmed, then I will acknowledge that confirmation and will let you know when it happens. Until then, I must humble myself before the Lord and avail myself to Him as I feel He is directing me."*

The question many people deal with is, *"What if I appear to be arrogant?"*

The core of our heart absolutely must contain deep humility as we proceed in our missions. We desire to be broken before the Lord and sensitive to him. The fear of God exists in a place of great humility and brokenness. The Word tells us that God resists the proud, and we certainly can't afford to allow that to happen!

Let me say it very clearly—we absolutely must proceed in our missions with BOTH humility AND boldness! There must be fire in our eyes and authority in our mouths as we push aside any obstacle that would hinder the valuable vision that God has entrusted us with!

God spoke to me the other day. He said, *"John, I have called you to be the guardian of my dream."*

Wow! I felt the weight of His dream for Manitou Springs. I have no option but to lay my life down for that dream. The boldness of the Holy Spirit consumes me when anything attempts to threaten God's plans. I was reminded that God is the one who knows my heart. If others presume me to be arrogant when God knows in my heart I am broken and undone before Him, that's OK. Remember, the devil is the accuser of the brethren. He will use any means possible to attack and to accuse. He is terrified of the fire of Heaven. He can't risk his kingdom being threatened by bold, authoritative fire-breathers who live their lives in the very presence of the Living God!

You know your heart. God knows your heart. God is your judge. Your goal is not to hesitate in the hopes that you *appear humble* as that can result in a compromised stance. Rather, you are to *be humble.* In this place of humility you have a responsibility to declare and lead with authority everything that God has given you.

We must deal with the fear of man's opinion of us. Are you afraid of people assuming you are prideful and arrogant? If so, even if your heart is truly humble, you won't deliver all of the messages that God entrusts to you. You won't lead as one with authority. You will fear the opinion of man and what comes out of your mouth will be filtered to match what you feel would be easiest and most comfortable for them to hear.

NO! We must not err on the side of timidity any more! Fear of conflict must be eradicated from the church and our lives! God has an offensive word, a divisive word, a word spoken with great fire and authority that must be declared to this generation!

Here's why this is an easy position to take: God judges our heart. If we are prideful, it's God's business and He is very good at dealing with us. We simply aren't called to *appear humble* so people don't talk about us. We are called to *be humble*–and boldly advance. If we are doing so with pride, just know that God has searched our heart and He will deal with us appropriately.

CHAPTER EIGHT

STEPS OF A RIGHTEOUS MAN

CAN WE STEP OUT WITH NO DIRECTION?

It's quite possible something precious has been lost in the corporate structure of most American churches, and most American's own lives. What has been gained is predictability, safety and clear communication of a desired goal. What has been lost? Courage. Risk. And, most of all, faith.

The addictive and safe qualities of a well "thought out" strategy are hard for many to ignore. After all, the more clearly we can share our goals in life, presumably the more people will support and understand us. That's important to many as they venture out into life. They want support. They want to be affirmed. *"Yes Johnny, that sure sounds like a great plan! We're all behind you! It should work like a charm!"*

In the previous paragraph I intentionally put the phrase "thought out" in quotes. In the west, it's most common to engage our minds first, and then our spirits. This process of decision making is terribly detrimental. When we allow our minds to filter divine instructions, we often will not experience the confirmation in our spirits. However, if we receive signals from the Holy Spirit in our spirits first, and then step out in blind faith, we will move much further down the road much more quickly. While human wisdom may say, *"Wait,"* our spirits are confirmed that it's time to move now! Flesh may cringe at such a quick move while our spirits are saying, *"Why wait?"* On the flip side, our spirits may cry *"Wait!"* while our flesh is impatient.

The issue comes when one person who is listening in his spirit shares what he is led to do with someone who may be analyzing it in their intellect. These are two different data streams and may be handled and filtered quite differently. Spiritual things can only be discerned spiritually. It seems foolish to our intellect. It's usually only after the fact that we will be able to explain much of the process to others. That revelation will be at least partially translatable in our minds. We'll be able to explain some of it, share it and testify to the greatness of God.

> *1 Corinthians 2:12-14 Now we have received, not the spirit of the world, but the Spirit who is from God, that we might know the things that have been freely given to us by God. These things we also speak, not in words which man's wisdom teaches but which the Holy Spirit teaches, comparing spiritual things with spiritual. But the natural man does not receive the things of the Spirit of God, for they are foolishness to him; nor can he know them, because they are spiritually discerned.*

This is an important Scripture. What God does simply cannot be known first in the natural. If this is the case, why do we demand an explanation in the natural? If it isn't supposed to make sense outside of our spirits, why do we even pursue intellectual understanding prior to spiritual reception?

Think about it this way. Signals to the mind and signals to the spirit are not simply on different frequencies, but they are two completely different mediums of communication. Just like audio and video are entirely different. If I am standing right next to a radio tower at a radio station there is no way I can know what is coming out of that tower. I can read the programming schedule. I can possibly watch the DJ through the window as he's on the air. But, that's about it. There are powerful radio waves blasting all around us, but we cannot receive them—unless we have a radio. Now, let's take it a bit further. Now I can turn on the radio and listen to beautiful music, announcements for the coming week and other information. I'm moved emotionally. Maybe I cried. Maybe I laughed. I'm blown away because I EXPERIENCED something at a level way beyond my intellect.

Now, to share this experience with someone is quite difficult. I could use great descriptive words like, *"Amazing!", "Powerful", "Passionate!"*

Of course, that just doesn't do it justice. So, let's bring this back into the arena of hearing God. As a leader I am to be intimately in tune with God's streaming audio. I'm moved to tears, full of passion, deeply expectant. I may get some strange directives that I am to share with the congregation. I'd know in my spirit how amazing this is, how peaceful it makes me, how joy just erupts. No matter the inconvenience, I know deep inside that this is it! The church must understand this. As a leader gets data in his spirit, he probably won't be able to communicate it well to the intellect or even the emotions. People who didn't experience what the leader experienced simply must trust that he or she really did experience God himself!

Many dreams and visions are never pursued because they simply don't make sense. They can't be explained. What if God told you to quit your job? He gave no other instructions. Just quit your job. Any number of issues would immediately arise. What would your wife think? What about the truth in the Word of God that those who don't work don't eat? What about the simple fact that it doesn't make sense? It would appear foolish to our friends. It appears to be a haphazard way to live. How would we pay our bills? And, simply, why would God want me to do that? What's the purpose? The simple answer is that, *"God said"* and He knows what He is doing.

You might say, *"That's ok for an individual, but you just can't lead others without explaining the process and gaining their agreement."*

Really? We could revisit the critical issue of church government here. *God's leaders in the Word of God rarely explained their reason for initiating obedience to God's instructions.* Those under their authority just responded to God's leaders who were responsible for their lives.

It may be simpler to investigate real stories in the Bible. Did God's leaders have it all figured out before they made decisions? Did they have to explain it well before people would follow? Or, did people simply follow their leader?

There is a verse that is often used when discussing unity, direction and agreement. Most people perceive this Scripture to display the art of democracy, compromise and concession. Here's the verse:

Amos 3:3 Can two walk together, unless they are agreed?

So, the train of thought usually is, *"Let's collaborate, let's compromise, let's discuss this and come to an agreed direction."*

This thought process doesn't line up with the prevailing principles of Scripture. Let's look a little further down in Amos:

Amos 3:7 Surely the Lord GOD does nothing, Unless He reveals His secret to His servants the prophets.

God speaks to people. He did yesterday and He does today. So, if God gives a directive to an individual, and agreement is required for unity and the fulfillment of the purpose, what is the appropriate train of thought in regard to Amos 3:3?

Submission.

I often say this in our church, *"If you are having a hard time hearing God, make sure you stick very close to people who do!"*

Additionally, if two people seemingly hear God differently, there's a simple resolution—the one under authority submits to the one in authority. Period. They then are agreed and can move ahead instead of debating back and forth and wasting precious moments as the end of time as we know it approaches.

As we look at this, ask this question: what would happen if your pastor announced to his church of 500 people that God gave him directions for the New Year. All programs are to be cancelled. Children are to sit with their parents on Sundays. The usual Sunday service will be cancelled in favor of waiting in silence for the next instructions from God. During the week we will be prayer walking the city Monday-Friday evenings. Saturdays are to be a day of refreshing and rest for your families.

What would happen? Would people respond to these instructions? Would they embrace lawlessness and become self-governing and decide what to respond to and what to ignore? Would they gossip about the pastor? Would they complain that it all makes no sense? Would they put a time limit on their involvement after which they must see fruit or they will leave? Would they put their family's desires ahead of responding to these instructions? Would they demand an explanation?

All of these things and more would occur. I propose that nothing short of complete submission and unity is critical and appropriate in times like this. Nothing immoral was suggested by the pastor. Nothing unscriptural. Yes, a lot of inconvenience, irritation, disagreement, frustration and disappointment may be in the picture... but that's ok! Remember–God would never cause us to violate His established government. He would never tell a servant to do something different than what his leader would. God may allow some conflict for the purpose of refining the church, but He would never cause anybody to disobey their authority, outside of directives that are clearly unbiblical.

So, did God ever give direction in Scripture without giving understanding of the process or the end result? Let's look:

> *Judges 7:15-18 And so it was, when Gideon heard the telling of the dream and its interpretation, that he worshipped. He returned to the camp of Israel, and said, "Arise, for the LORD has delivered the camp of Midian into your hand." Then he divided the three hundred men into three companies, and he put a trumpet into every man's hand, with empty pitchers, and torches inside the pitchers. And he said to them, "Look at me and do likewise; watch, and when I come to the edge of the camp you shall do as I do: "When I blow the trumpet, I and all who are with me, then you also blow the trumpets on every side of the whole camp, and say, 'The sword of the LORD and of Gideon!'"*

Any normal person would have laughed and then asked, *"What in the world are you thinking?"*

> *Judges 7:20 Then the three companies blew the trumpets and broke the pitchers--they held the torches in their left*

*hands and the trumpets in their right hands for blowing--
and they cried, "The sword of the LORD and of Gideon!"*

But, blowing trumpets and shouting and breaking things and holding torches was the order of the Lord, and it worked! The 300 men didn't question Gideon. They simply responded.

> *Joshua 6:3-5 "You shall march around the city, all you men of war; you shall go all around the city once. This you shall do six days. "And seven priests shall bear seven trumpets of rams' horns before the ark. But the seventh day you shall march around the city seven times, and the priests shall blow the trumpets. "It shall come to pass, when they make a long blast with the ram's horn, and when you hear the sound of the trumpet, that all the people shall shout with a great shout; then the wall of the city will fall down flat. And the people shall go up every man straight before him."*

Yes, Joshua said the city will fall down flat, but the directives were nonsensical! It made no sense whatsoever! How does marching and blowing trumpets translate into stone walls falling down? How? God's ways are simply not our ways. That's why we cannot lean on our own understanding. We must expect to hear God give us some radical instructions.

Pastors– Lead! Go!

Christians– Follow! Go!

We need to be in order, in rank, in submission, in obedience and excited about the journey!

> *John 9:6-7 When He had said these things, He spat on the ground and made clay with the saliva; and He anointed the eyes of the blind man with the clay. And He said to him, "Go, wash in the pool of Siloam" (which is translated, Sent). So he went and washed, and came back seeing.*

Jesus did something very bizarre. And, you'll notice He didn't tell the man why he put mud in his eyes. He didn't tell him why he should wash in the pool. He didn't even tell the man he would see again!

We could go on and on. God will very often give radical directives that make no sense. All we have to do is learn to hear His voice, listen to the prophets, submit to our authority and enjoy a constant supernatural life!

CHAPTER NINE

GOD SAID

There is a part of my heart that is broken. There is a part of my spirit that has been riled up. Irritated. Why? The more I talk with Christians, with pastors, with leaders, with others who have made Jesus a priority in their lives, the more I get blank stares when I talk about God speaking.

God said. We've all heard it before. In America we are so skeptical, so worried, analytical, thoughtful, that the idea of God saying anything at all seems far fetched. Especially when someone uses that irritating two word phrase in response to the question, *"Why did you do that?"*

God said.

I wonder if Paul had a similar issue that caused him to say, *"Follow me as I follow Christ!"*

He was confident in his ability to hear and to obey. He understood that others had yet to hone the skill of hearing a supernatural voice.

But, this dilemma is worse than what we have already discussed. Instead of daily hearing the voice of God, gaining fresh new instructions and having the ride of our lives, we are forced into corners daily with demands of formulaic reasoning to explain our positions.

I have no position–God said.

Pastors, how can we presume anybody in the church, people on our boards, Sunday school teachers, trustees, can clearly understand an earth-shaking vision of God... that was specifically and personally given to the leader? How can they understand why we might make a decision to cancel a program or switch gears? It makes no sense! The math doesn't add up!

Let's get used to it–when God moves, the math simply doesn't add up. People will be inconvenienced. Explanations won't be sufficient. Agendas will be tampered with. God does things very differently than us.

I can hear the defense now–*"Well, God would never do anything that would cause the senior leadership to not be on board with! He would ensure everybody agreed in the Spirit. It would feel good to everyone involved, or at least the key people."*

Wow. When did the church become democratic? I often hear that leaders must not be dictators. Really? What is a king then? We are in a kingdom, not a democracy. Leaders must lead with boldness and confidence as they will be held responsible for their assignments. Leaders must realize that if they have anything fresh at all, MOST of what they do will ruffle feathers! They will cut across the grain. It won't make sense and it will irritate many!

Most leaders aren't willing to take their families through the pain of radical disagreement within the ranks of the sheep and other shepherds. Bold leaders receive many negative and discouraging emails, many 'urgent' phone calls. They lose people who disapprove regularly. Gossip runs wild. People exalt themselves above their shepherd. They fall in love with their own opinions. They gain consensus which masquerades as correctness.

I was at Jimmy Swaggart's confession in 1988. I was a student in the Bible college. I believe the greatest victory the enemy had was not the collapse of a world-wide ministry that was seeing thousands upon thousands saved. It wasn't embarrassing shame on the church. It was when he caused Christians, who were once deeply submitted to leadership, to embrace lawlessness that resulted from a new found lack of trust. Self-government. I believe many made the decision, *"I won't be hurt again! I won't be abused again! I will no longer submit to pastoral leadership. I'll keep control in my court. I'll decide who I follow and for how long. I'll govern my own life."*

It was a dark day for the American church.

We see people leaving churches daily without receiving the blessing of the pastor. People don't respond to the challenge of church leadership. We go as far as we and we alone decide.

I use an example to make this point clear. I lead Revolution House of Prayer. Last week was probably the most exciting week in our history. We had prayed countless hours, made preparations, rearranged schedules and were very excited about a team of 21 people who were coming to serve with us from Michigan. The pastor of this group is an amazing friend. They were coming largely because I ministered at a retreat in Michigan last year and they were excited to experience our ministry. I was excited to see them, more than they will ever know. It was a big deal. Now, as a man under authority, I am submitted to my overseers. Let's say one of the overseers called me. He said, *"John, a pastor in Alabama is going through some difficulties. He'll be out of the pulpit for an indefinite period of time. I need you to fly there immediately to fill that pulpit and to help steady that church."*

Yikes! But, God had used me to put together this very important week! I need to be at home! My friend is counting on me to be there! I would certainly have the freedom to share my concerns with my overseer. I could emphasize the significance of this very important week. We could discuss this in depth.

After the conversation, let's presume my overseer said, *"John, I appreciate your situation, but I am still impressed you are the one to fly to Alabama. I need you to go."*

Now, let me make this very clear. I WOULD HAVE NO DECISION TO MAKE. I would have no choice. I would have nothing to pray about. I would be on a plane the very next day.

Why? He is my leader. I submit to him. You may ask, *"But what if God says one thing to you and your spiritual leader says another?"*

Good question. Here's a good answer–God NEVER calls us to violate His established authority! He puts every person in authority. God is big enough to work through conflicts. He has proven himself in dealing with all types of leaders–good and evil. He is to make things work out, not us! We are never to be self-governing. We submit always. The only exception is if someone were to cause us to violate a very clear biblical truth. That's it.

Leaders can't easily lead today because all of us have, to one degree or another, violated biblical church government. It's a submission issue. It's a brokenness issue. It's a love issue. Leaders will ask us to go with them to some new places via some unintelligible methods. All they can say is, *"God said."* We must respond! Read Joshua chapter 3. Joshua heard God directly, gave the orders and everybody was in position. Because of this, they entered the Promised Land! Further submission to some goofy instructions of God, through Joshua, caused the walls of Jericho to fall!

I am guessing that Joshua, as a great leader, didn't have a "my way or the highway" attitude. But, there was unquestionably a "my way or the desert" reality. Moses allowed a democratic spirit to enter into the camp when the spies were given the power of decision. The majority agreed that it was not a good idea to enter the Promised Land. They experienced the reality of the desert to the degree that death visited them there. To embrace a democratic and independent spirit, and to remove oneself from a position of quick response to God's directives through His leaders results in tragedy.

Keep reading throughout the book of Joshua and you'll see what happens when people removed themselves from a submissive relationship with Gods man Joshua. It's devastating.

> *Joshua 6:18-19 "And you, by all means abstain from the accursed things, lest you become accursed when you take of the accursed things, and make the camp of Israel a curse, and trouble it. "But all the silver and gold, and vessels of bronze and iron, are consecrated to the LORD; they shall come into the treasury of the LORD."*

We see a directive of Joshua here. He gave specific orders on how to handle the spoils. Don't touch the accursed things and bring all of the silver and gold to the treasury of the Lord.

> *Joshua 7:1 But the children of Israel committed a trespass regarding the accursed things, for Achan the son of Carmi, the son of Zabdi, the son of Zerah, of the tribe of Judah, took of the accursed things; so the anger of the LORD burned against the children of Israel.*

Joshua 7:3-12 And they returned to Joshua and said to him, "Do not let all the people go up, but let about two or three thousand men go up and attack Ai. Do not weary all the people there, for the people of Ai are few." So about three thousand men went up there from the people, but they fled before the men of Ai. And the men of Ai struck down about thirty-six men, for they chased them from before the gate as far as Shebarim, and struck them down on the descent; therefore the hearts of the people melted and became like water. Then Joshua tore his clothes, and fell to the earth on his face before the ark of the LORD until evening, he and the elders of Israel; and they put dust on their heads. And Joshua said, "Alas, Lord GOD, why have You brought this people over the Jordan at all--to deliver us into the hand of the Amorites, to destroy us? Oh, that we had been content, and dwelt on the other side of the Jordan! "O Lord, what shall I say when Israel turns its back before its enemies? "For the Canaanites and all the inhabitants of the land will hear it, and surround us, and cut off our name from the earth. Then what will You do for Your great name?" So the LORD said to Joshua: "Get up! Why do you lie thus on your face? "Israel has sinned, and they have also transgressed My covenant which I commanded them. For they have even taken some of the accursed things, and have both stolen and deceived; and they have also put it among their own stuff. "Therefore the children of Israel could not stand before their enemies, but turned their backs before their enemies, because they have become doomed to destruction. Neither will I be with you anymore, unless you destroy the accursed from among you.

Again, God's promise of advancing His children was delayed, much like it was in the desert, because of disobedience. We simply must hear and obey God with great precision, even if His directives may seem difficult, strange or nonsensical.

It's time we as the church realize that God is ready to give some crazy instructions! He wants to blow away our wisdom! What was done in the past is done! What is to be done can't be measured by past wisdom or even recent successes!

Let me say it simply—What God will do in these end times will cause us to flinch and squirm and break. Our flesh will despise it. Our minds will be mesmerized by it. But, His amazing end time plan will come to pass, through you and me. The question is, will we have the courage to listen in on God's board meeting? It will shatter our thinking and renew us like we could never dream.

CHAPTER TEN

HEARING PROBLEMS

The more I focus on my primary calling to share the amazing life of experiencing God in every moment of our lives, and the more I gain insight from those in churches around the nation who don't consider this to be a driving force of their ministries, the more I grow uneasy.

There seems to be a radical lack of understanding of what it is to be with God, to hear God and to experience God. This is not simply a mark of the difference between Charismatics and mainline denominations. This is dangerous!

I often emphasize that I am a *city church guy*. I love the variety of expressions of the body of Christ. But, to not be wildly intimate with God (and I'm talking about church leaders here) is a hazardous place to be. I don't know how many church growth strategies I've heard that have nothing to do with actually gaining new insight from God himself. How can God do a new thing if we are relying on old material in the latest books?

Leaders must hear God to lead! Period! Why? If they don't hear God, if they don't get their instructions from the source, then they aren't really leading. They will then rely on leaning on others through books, through a church vote or through gaining a consensus. They will lead by committee. That's not leadership. Votes, committees, books–they all rely on 'proven strategies'.

To make future decisions based on old wine is foolishness! Sure, we can glean parts of the puzzle. We can gain practical wisdom. BUT, if we read the Bible we'll quickly see that God's great leaders didn't rely on past info. The paved new ground!

To rely on a vote or consensus will result in:

- Decisions that err on the side of safety
- Attempting to duplicate what has already been done
- Very little risk
- No vision
- Decisions that perpetuate the comfort zone instead of initiating challenge

When God calls a single person to listen to His voice, as a wild leader, this will result in:

- Dreams
- Visions
- Offending the flesh
- Huge risk
- Relying on the impossible for success to be realized

- Destroying the status quo
- Boldness
- Passion
- Expectancy
- Humility as reliance on God is a must

I could go on and on. Bottom line—leaders, pray double-digit hours every week! Hear God! Don't rely on gaining a second hand opinion when you can get first hand instructions from God himself!

If we are going to go where nobody has gone before, there is no other way.

The more of the Holy Spirit we experience, the more mere human effort seems nearly futile. I've been in the church for most of my life. I've been around most every type of program, ministry and good idea. These programs are certainly not inherently wrong... but, the question is, *is there power surging through them?*

Many have made a conscious decision to follow Jesus. They agree with the Word of God. They subscribe to its directives. They desire the blessings. However, when a person is not living a life that is in revival, literally endued with power, their human efforts become tiring and burdensome.

For example, it's one thing to evangelize door-to-door and hope someone will say the sinner's prayer and it's entirely another thing to be intoxicated by the Holy Spirit to the point that there is fire in our eyes and a wildly accurate prophetic word for a lost person coming out of our mouths!

It's one thing to encourage and pray for a sick person and quite another to declare the exact will of God and heal that person on the spot.

It's one thing to learn how to be a better Christian by studying the Bible and it's another to actually live out the impossible directives of the Word of God as the Holy Spirit blows through you!

It's one thing to come up with great object lessons for a teaching and it's totally another to receive crystal clear dreams and visions!

There is a level, a dimension that is SO EASILY AVAILABLE to every one of us! I'm 37 years old. I don't have as much time left on Earth as I thought I did as a teenager when life seemed like an eternity. I want to experience as much God as I am supposed to in the next 50 or so years… before it's time to go home. I want more power, more anointing, more dreams, more vision, more love, more effectiveness, more passion!

Time is short–it's time NOW to seek God continually! I need to pray more than I ever have in my life! If I don't, I'll miss so much!

This world doesn't need another nice little Bible study or Sunday school class or nifty Christian T-shirt. The world needs to see radical joy, demonstrations of power, fire in our eyes and the supernatural love of God himself blazing through us.

Let's just do it.

CHAPTER ELEVEN

REVELATION DRIVEN PRAYER

STOP! YOU'RE PRAYING WRONG!

That's what God told me one day as I was in some deep prayer. I was currently working part-time at a call center. I had been fairly frustrated that I wasn't able to leave that job so I could work full-time in the church.

That day, I was praying from a place of frustration. *"God, oh God, please grow the church! Let the finances increase! Please God!"*

That was when, as clear as a bell, I heard God say, *"Stop! You're praying wrong!"*

What? How could that be? I was praying so hard. As I walked around the 1000 square feet of sanctuary space in the early days of Revolution I really felt like I was doing well. Didn't God want the church to grow? Didn't He want to provide for our needs?

Then God said something I'll never forget. *"You are praying as if I'm resisting you. Don't you realize I put those desires in your heart? Why are you begging me for a desire that I initiated? I gave you the desire in the first place!"*

Wow! That ruined my whole perception of what prayer was! I had to think differently.

God then said, *"There is one who IS resisting you though. The enemy doesn't want these desires I placed in your heart to come to pass. It is the enemy whom you must fight."*

So, I launched into a new dimension of faith filled and violent prayer!

I felt impressed that God wanted me to practice this new revelation he gave me on prayer. He told me He wanted me to have more time to pray and initiate revival in the city. He wanted me to quit my job at the call center. I had captured the heart of God and I knew it was my turn to enforce His will. The enemy must move!

"In the powerful name of Jesus Christ, I command you devil to release! Get off of my schedule! I declare the heart of God is for me to quit my job and to advance His Kingdom full time in Manitou Springs! How dare you touch the plans of God!"

> *1 John 5:14-15 Now this is the confidence that we have in Him, that if we ask anything according to His will, He hears us. And if we know that He hears us, whatever we ask, we know that we have the petitions that we have asked of Him.*

I prayed according to His will. He wanted me to work full-time in the ministry. One week later, as a church of about 35 people, we received a check in the Sunday offering for $50,000. The following week we received $25,000.

I was full time two weeks later.

That money was "more than enough" for me to go full-time at the church. We also used it to get into our current building. God wanted us to have that all along. The enemy didn't. I was praying wrong. I was praying as if the provision had to be coaxed away from God. In reality, God had already released it and I just had to go get it—and blast through the enemy's resistance on the way.

That's why it's critical to be people of prayer. *How else can we know what God wants us to pray for?* What to stand on. What not to focus on. What to delay? We must hear Him!

Of course, the primary thrust of this entire book is hearing the ever-present voice of God. Let me at this point also emphasize the seemingly obvious power of the written Word of God. The revelation of Revelation Driven Prayer has literally changed my life in many realms and dimensions. The above story revealed a process I went through with regard to God's will for that moment of my life. He spoke specifically to me regarding His desires.

Another story, though very short, had an equal impact upon my life. I was once again in a place of 'frustration prayer'. I was crying out for my needs to be met. I was banging on the doors of heaven in passionate prayer for finances, among other things. Once again I heard the voice of God deep within my spirit, *"Your prayer is hindering you."* What? Did I hear what I thought I heard? God told me that my prayer in that moment was doing more damage than good. I should stop if I planned on continuing in that vein.

He then said, *"Without faith it is impossible to please me."* He added, *"Doubt in prayer will ensure that prayer goes unanswered."* Ok, He had my attention. I pondered this, and wrestled with these issues. I didn't want to doubt. I wanted more than anything to be a man of faith. I wanted these pieces to fit together so I could arrive at some conclusion. God was telling me not to pray! Yet, I still had unresolved issues that demanded a miracle. Oh how alone I felt!

Then the answer came. *God asked me why I was praying for something that was already promised in His Word.* He has promised to supply all of my needs according to His riches in glory. *The very act of asking God for my needs to be met revealed my lack of faith that it has already been done!* Wow! I was attempting to convince God to do something that He already had resolved! *My prayer evidenced my doubt* which resulted in my prayer being unanswered!

> *Mark 11:24 Therefore I say to you, whatever things you ask when you pray, believe that you receive them, and you will have them.*

No begging, no coercing, no convincing, no doubting allowed in prayer!

> *James 1:5-8 If any of you lacks wisdom, let him ask of God, who gives to all liberally and without reproach, and it will be given to him. But let him ask in faith, with no doubting, for he who doubts is like a wave of the sea driven and tossed by the wind. For let not that man suppose that he will receive anything from the Lord; he is a double-minded man, unstable in all his ways.*

Now, when I pray, I simply remember that *prayer* rhymes with *declare*. I don't have an *addiction to petition*. I hear God and then declare to the atmosphere and my situations how they must conform to His will. It turns us from a position of defeat and passivity to a position of victory and spiritual violence and powerful faith! We change from the afflicted to the afflictor!

We had a team of college aged young men and women come to Revolution for Mission Manitou–a spiritual warfare missions experience. It was an amazing week. The highlight of the week was 'prayer in a cave'. From time to time we'll have prayer teams join us for four hours of non-stop worship, prayer, prophecy, intercession and passion. We are literally in a large cave, in perfect darkness with no sense of time. It's an experiment in *Revelation Driven Prayer*. This particular night was a night I'll never forget. For nearly a year I had suffered from a severe pinched nerve in my right shoulder. My right arm and fingers would either tingle or go numb continually. My shoulder, at times, hurt so badly I could barely stand it. I had been to a chiropractor and a massage therapist. Neither worked.

Prior to entering the cave, we had a powerful prayer and worship event at Revolution. Near the end of that service, I had asked one of the prayer missionaries from Michigan to pray for my shoulder. This particular girl had been pressing so hard the entire week as God was healing her, touching her and shaking her. She craved breakthrough in her life. She prayed for me for quite some time, and then it was time for all of us to enter the cave. I didn't experience a healing, though I was blessed that she took the time to pray for me.

In the cave, we experienced four seasons that the Lord established as a part of the *Revelation Driven Prayer* training program.

REVELATION DRIVEN PRAYER STEP ONE: ELIMINATION

First, we repented. We eliminated everything from the depths of our heart. Complete surrender. Remember, it's perfectly dark in the cave. You can't see your hand in front of your face. People's cries were echoing thorough the cavern. People who never had the confidence to cry out or to pray out in public were wonderfully released to do so. There was such a presence of the Holy Spirit as people wept and repented and released past hurts.

The stronger the Holy Spirit stirs the more we crave to eliminate and repent deeply. The groanings of a broken and humbled person simply overwhelm people who are pressing intentionally and passionately into the place where God is moving.

> *2 Chronicles 7:13-15 When I shut up heaven and there is no rain, or command the locusts to devour the land, or send pestilence among My people, if My people who are called by My name will humble themselves, and pray and seek My face, and turn from their wicked ways, then I will hear from heaven, and will forgive their sin and heal their land. Now My eyes will be open and My ears attentive to prayer made in this place.*

This season is often difficult for some to press through, but it's the most critical time we'll spend. The reason many people's prayer life is so frustrating is because the necessary sacrifice of time hasn't been made. Pressing into a place of repentance results in a lot of time being made undone before our Father. If we humble ourselves, pray and seek we'll discover God's favor. Seeking takes time. Lengthy prayer simply must be a normal reality on a continual basis if we desire to break through to the heart of God.

> *Psalms 34:17-18 The righteous cry out, and the Lord hears, And delivers them out of all their troubles. The Lord is near to those who have a broken heart, And saves such as have a contrite spirit.*

This is what we found in the cave–people crying out! If we go to a deeply expressive place of repentance, desperation, desire and longing for our Lover, our Lover will hear us! If our heart is broken, He is near to us! That is one amazing Scripture!

However, so often our prayers are thrown up to heaven almost in passing without any brokenness at all, and we wonder why God isn't responsive to us in the way the Word of God describes.

We'll often hear people yelling at the top of their lungs, *"God I need You! Jesus, come into my life like never before! Please, fire of God, burn my flesh!"*

We'll also hear people repenting of anything from apathy to mocking to abuse. People want to be free from their unwitting alliance with the enemy. They don't want to be lukewarm, arrogant, insecure, suspicious or defeated in any way. This season of elimination causes us all to be emptied. Deliverance happens at times in this phase. People of all types, ages and maturity find themselves craving to have every hindrance removed from their lives so they can actually see God, right there in a place of perfect darkness,

On this particular cave experience, after an hour or so of pouring our hearts out to God we moved into the next phase–*Consecration.*

REVELATION DRIVEN PRAYER STEP TWO: CONSECRATION

This is a time of adoration, worship and becoming aligned as perfectly as possible with Christ Jesus. It was beautiful to hear the raw worship sounding off the walls of the cavern. After finding themselves empty after the previous season, people were longing to be full of a supernatural fire. God was closer than ever!

> *Romans 12:1-2 I beseech you therefore, brethren, by the mercies of God, that you present your bodies a living sacrifice,*

*holy, acceptable to God, which is your reasonable service.
And do not be conformed to this world, but be transformed
by the renewing of your mind, that you may prove what is
that good and acceptable and perfect will of God.*

This second season is critical if we are to clearly hear God in the next season. As we find ourselves emptied of past sins, issues and mind-sets, we can now simply say, *"Father, here am I, send me!"*

Instead of desiring to warm our flesh by the fire of God's presence, we lay our bodies, as living sacrifices, directly on the fire and cry out, *"Consume us God!"*

We tell God that our lives are in His hands. If He desires for us to be martyred for His cause, then that's what we want. If He wants us to step into a certain mission, that's what we will do. Our lives are no longer our own, but we are surrendered to God. We are consecrated to Him. We're excited about what God can do through a completely yielded vessel.

This season is marked by a lot of excitement and wonderful freedom. The result of eliminating all of our baggage is a bunch of extra room for God to operate in our lives. The Spirit of God literally fills us up to overflowing, and we are suddenly putty in His hands.

We may go on for a couple of hours in this season. We'll worship, weep, experience the baptism of the Holy Spirit, pray boldly in tongues, continually break in His presence and fall deeply in love with Him. It's simply amazing. Now, with the old man crucified and the Spirit of God blowing like a wind in and through us, it becomes very easy to hear His voice. We capture His dreams and desires for our lives.

This next season is critical to the process of Revelation Driven Prayer–hearing God. *Revelation.*

REVELATION DRIVEN PRAYER STEP THREE: REVELATION

With this team from Michigan, I encouraged people, most of whom have never prophesied, to listen to the voice of God and share it with us. One by one people would share pictures, impressions, Scriptures and other words from heaven. I explained that God desires to speak clearly and continually to every man, woman and child of His on the planet.

> *1 Corinthians 14:1 Pursue love, and desire spiritual gifts, but especially that you may prophesy.*

To prophesy is simply to hear God and to repeat what He says. Share with others the heartbeat of God in any given situation. Hearing God is one of the most exciting parts of one's personal experience as a Christian. We are all to have spiritual dreams and visions, to walk in the Spirit and hear in the Spirit. God is continually sharing His heart with us and to receive that data from the invisible realm is amazing!

Not only does it make life exciting, it makes it survivable. The only way we can obey God is if we hear Him! So, as we hear His voice, we can know what is required of us. We can see into the spirit realm and understand how to battle the enemy. This is how it unfolded in this particular situation:

We were about to move into the fourth and last season called *execution–declaring and enforcing the will of God* that was just revealed in this season of prophetic revelation. All of a sudden, I heard this sweet voice from on the other side of the cavern call out, *"John?"* I said, *"Yes?"* She said, *"I just can't go on until I share something with you."* It was the same girl who had prayed for my shoulder back at Revolution.

"God is squeezing my heart. It's so strong and I have to share it with you." *"It's not good though."* Oh boy! Here we go. One of those moments that every leader has to deal with at one time or another–a crazy prophetic word!

I told her, *"Ok, go ahead and share it. Let's see what God has to tell us."* It was important to me to encourage her in this as it was obviously a critical moment for her. She was hearing God, and I was excited about that. She went on to tell me that she saw a vision when she was praying for me back at Revolution, but she didn't know how to share it. That same vision intensified extensively during the season of prophecy and hearing God there in the cave. She saw someone holding a voodoo doll of me and they were poking me in the shoulder over and over again.

Now, what she didn't know was that I was there in the dark on the other side of the room wincing in extreme pain for the previous four hours. I was contorting my body every which way I could in an attempt to relieve the pressure in my shoulder. I was almost in tears much of the night.

I then announced to everybody there that we were a living experiment. God was taking us by the hand and teaching us about *Revelation Driven Prayer.* I told everybody that God has revealed His desire–He wanted me healed that very moment. It was now time to move into our last season–*execution.*

REVELATION DRIVEN PRAYER STEP FOUR: EXECUTION

I asked that girl if she would pray for me. Wow! Something happened to this girl–the fire of God was on her! She prayed down the heavens while the rest of the people in that cave warred in the Spirit and interceded with passion. The noise was astounding.

All of a sudden my shoulder started to burn intensely! It was like someone poured hot oil on my shoulder and was rubbing it in. It went down my arm all the way to the tips of my fingers. God was instantly healing me. I went through every movement I could think of, I pressed my fingers deep into the spot that had previously hurt so badly. My fingers which were previously partially numb were now highly sensitive. It was really happening–I was healed! My arm was on fire. I told everybody what was going on as it was happening. I half-way jokingly asked them if they could see my arm glowing there in the dark cave! It was so hot I thought people around me could feel the warmth!

To this very day my arm has been healed. God was waiting to heal me so all of those people in that dark cave would experience the glory of God.

> *John 9:1-3 Now as Jesus passed by, He saw a man who was blind from birth. And His disciples asked Him, saying, "Rabbi, who sinned, this man or his parents, that he was born blind?" Jesus answered, "Neither this man nor his parents sinned, but that the works of God should be revealed in him.*

This last season of execution is simply that–we execute the instructions of God as He reveals them to us. He didn't have anything else for us to do at that moment, and our ability to hear Him clearly kept us from praying amiss. We came into perfect agreement with God, looked at the spirit of Infirmity with fire in our eyes and a supernatural confidence and cast it out. The attack of witchcraft was annihilated in a place of agreed prayer. We executed God's instructions that were revealed to a repentant and consecrated people who were filled with the fire of the Holy Spirit.

Revelation Driven Prayer works. We pour ourselves out, spend hours in the presence of God, hear His voice and then war in the Spirit. Miracles are then the expected, and very regular, result.

> *John 15:7-8 If you abide in Me, and My words abide in you, you will ask what you desire, and it shall be done for you. By this My Father is glorified, that you bear much fruit; so you will be My disciples.*

I want to encourage you to pattern your own prayer life in this way. Every day, present yourself to the Lord and go through these four seasons. If Christians will eagerly step up to a place of two or three hours of intentional prayer every day, we will experience an outpouring of God within weeks if not sooner!

I find myself exhilarated when my time in the prayer room is dosed with waves of insight into God's heart. It's becomes easy to hit my face, cry out in pursuit of the Living God and then to press on into hours of prayer–when it's fueled by revelation.

When the cry of our heart is to discover the cry of God's heart, life in the invisible realm of prayer ramps up powerfully.

I believe the prayer movement will become the thrill ride that it's meant to be when it becomes predominantly a prophetic movement. Praying prayers into the nether regions without at least a low level of supernatural insight is a frustrating activity. It's a prime reason many people are resistant to a life of prayer.

> *Ephesians 5:15-17 Be very careful, then, how you live--not as unwise but as wise, making the most of every opportunity, because the days are evil. Therefore do not be foolish, but understand what the Lord's will is.*

The Holy Spirit schooled me in the important concept of effective and efficient prayer one day when I was alone in prayer at Revolution Church at the base of Pikes Peak in Manitou Springs, Colorado. Keep in mind that I have always been a 'prayer guy'. I caught the fire of love for Jesus in my early years when I was in the place of prayer and that hunger for intimacy with God has never ceased. This particular day I found myself praying very good prayers… but these particular prayers weren't on God's agenda for me that day. I was praying for church growth, for people that came to mind, for strategic ideas and other good and important topics. However, they were topics that came to mind based on human insight and yesterday's revelation. I had no leading that those focuses were also God's focus for me in that moment. I was praying blindly.

> *Ephesians 1:15-18 Therefore I also, after I heard of your faith in the Lord Jesus and your love for all the saints, do not cease to give thanks for you, making mention of you in my prayers: that the God of our Lord Jesus Christ, the Father of glory, may give to you the spirit of wisdom and revelation in the knowledge of Him, the eyes of your understanding being enlightened; that you may know what is the hope of His calling, what are the riches of the glory of His inheritance in the saints…*

Understand, blind prayers aren't bad. It's a very good thing to intercede for any number of pressing issues. However, I was learning that prayers based on human insight alone were simply not efficient. This particular day something else was on God's heart and he was instructing me to avoid distraction—even honorable distraction such as praying for people in the church—and to have laser precision by praying what was on God's heart. Prayer is all about agreement. If God's calling us to stand in the gap for one thing and we're focusing on another thing we are actually misaligned. Again, let me make it clear so people don't fall into guilt or false ideas. To pray is good and beneficial. However, we should crave the highest level of efficiency and effectiveness as possible. That's certainly God's desire.

A quick way to become disillusioned and discouraged in the place of prayer is to become plagued with what I call *petitionitis* or to discover *addiction to petition*. The thought that God is simply waiting for us to ask him for something so he can perform it for us is exceedingly short sighted. We should discuss our desires with God, but the idea that this is the limit of prayer is tragically flawed. Yes, we can ask God for things, but the adventure begins when we allow God to reveal his requests to us.

It simply makes sense to fuel our prayers with the revelation of what God is working on with us at that moment. One of the most exciting questions we can ask God is, *"What are you thinking about right now?"* If God revealed that a terrorist attack is scheduled to be carried out in our city within the next twelve hours, and he is attempting to reveal instructions for intercession on that issue it wouldn't make sense to spend precious time praying for other things.

This lesson was drilled home by the Holy Spirit this particular day at Revolution a few years ago. God said, *"Don't pray about anything until I reveal my agenda. Spend time preparing your heart to receive and to be an instrument of intercession and authority in my hands."*

This was one of the most important instructions I have ever received. The reality that God has such an expansive perspective that goes far beyond our own viewpoint should grip us.

> *Job 11:7 "Can you fathom the mysteries of God? Can you probe the limits of the Almighty?"*

*Romans 11:33 Oh, the depth of the riches of the wisdom
and knowledge of God!*

So, I walked around Revolution Church with no list of petitions. I worshiped, humbled my heart, prayed in tongues and waited.

God then spoke (this is always the starting point of effective
prayer). *"John, I don't want you to pray for anything else except for this
property. It's strategic and I want you to advance. It's time to take new
ground."*

The faith, anointing and presence of God increased immediately in such measure that it literally felt like the room was flooded to
the ceiling. Immediately after, my staff started to arrive for our weekly
staff meeting and one of them walked right up to me after he came
through the front door and said, *"What's going on? The faith is so high
in this room that you could cut it with a knife."*

He felt it as he walked through the door.

I shared with the team what God had instructed us to do. We
all spread out, prayed and anointed the property from room to room.
The city of Manitou Springs and this particular property has a very
dark history. Many call Manitou Springs the darkest and most strategi-
cally demonic city in the nation. This particular property was over 100
years old and was once a brothel. Revolution Church (now Revolution
House of Prayer) occupied about 2/3rds of the property and the owner
had his Moroccan restaurant in the other 1/3rd. A single wall divided
the two sides.

When the church first moved in to this location I found it
very hard to physically breathe. The demonic stronghold there was
unusually heavy. We did a good job of cleaning things up on our side
of the wall and enjoyed the presence of God in freedom to a wonderful

degree. However, this very day God was calling us to advance beyond the wall.

After we spent some time praying throughout the rooms of the building on our side, I called everybody together and told them we were to lay hands on the wall that divided the two sides and to pray from the perspective of authority and with great faith and confidence based on the revelation that God had given us.

Now, I hadn't spoken to my landlord for quite some time. We didn't cross paths very often, so what was about to happen was very much out of the ordinary.

As we were all praying, my cell phone rang. I just let it go to voicemail as we continued on. Then, something snapped. One of my elders looked at me and said, *"It's done. There's no reason to keep praying."*

I felt it too. It was awesome. We all went outside and walked around the perimeter of the building and thanked God for what was accomplished. At that point I remembered that I missed a phone call when I was inside praying at the wall, so I checked my voicemail. It was my landlord. He wanted to talk with me. Immediately the anointing around me started to burn even hotter.

I went to meet him and he asked, *"I was wondering if your church would you like to move in to the other side of the property?"*

I'm sure my face was white. The swirl of God was so strong on me that I had to intentionally maintain my composure. I said, *"Yes."*

I often joke that many people simply want God to call them on the phone with answers to their prayer… and for us, it kind of happened like that! Right in the middle of a powerfully unified and faith-filled moment of prayer my phone rang with the answer I was seeking!

That next month we moved into the very room that was on the other side of the wall where we were praying. Plus, our monthly rent was decreased from $8000 to $6000! We took ground and prospered financially all because I laid down my agenda, waited, received precise revelation and came into active agreement with it.

> *1 Cor 1:25 Because the foolishness of God is wiser than men, and the weakness of God is stronger than men.*

I am actively contending that the dry seasons of struggle in the prayer room that has weighed on so many will not remain the norm. The cry is for regular, perpetual revelation to rain down from heaven on a continual basis. If we are to walk in the Spirit, we must have the ability to see and hear and discern in the Spirit.

Instead of simply praying along with the prayer leader in the room for the nation of Egypt, for example, we'll receive, on both a personal and a corporate level, clear and active revelation about Egypt or whatever is on God's agenda for that session. The more people that receive a strong 'yes' in their spirit as intercession is being led, the more agreed they are and the more effective it is.

It's good to pray for what seems obvious any time of the day. It's better to pray in a specific moment for whatever issue God's calling us to focus on. The goal is to lay the list aside as much as possible and wait until God tells us exactly what to agree on. We'll find ourselves more alive, refreshed and strengthened as we ride on that wave instead of pressing ahead without it.

As we minimize our agendas and expect God to give us precise instructions for prayer we'll see the testimonies sky rocket around the world.

CHAPTER TWELVE

WE'VE NEVER BEEN THIS WAY BEFORE

Man follows man. There is a significant problem with that. Yes, absolutely, we are to "follow Paul as he follows Christ." Yes, we should have spiritual heroes. Yes, we should definitely submit to and serve others. Yes, God has given us an authority structure here on Earth.

But! There is one absolutely fatal mistake that believers make day after day. This fatal mistake results in unfulfilled missions. It results in living an average life. It results in low self-esteem. It destroys confidence.

The mistake? Not understanding that we nor anybody has ever been this way before! What way? Our personal destiny! Our mission! Our dreams and visions!

I believe the reason for the lack of dreams and visions and prophetic words in most believer's lives is that they are in a strangle hold of the enemy of doubt, fear and loss of hope. After all, how can we dream God sized dreams if we know, we just know, that our friends and family won't believe in us?

> *Joshua 3:2-4 So it was, after three days, that the officers went through the camp; and they commanded the people, saying, "When you see the ark of the covenant of the LORD your God, and the priests, the Levites, bearing it, then you shall set out from your place and go after it. "Yet there shall be a space between you and it, about two thousand cubits by measure. Do not come near it, that you may know the way by which you must go, for you have not passed this way before."*

Now, that's good leadership–telling people to WATCH GOD. Keep their eyes on the Ark of the Covenant, which is the very presence of God. Watch where it moves, when it moves, how fast it moves AND GO AFTER IT! Why is that so important? Why must we be radically attentive to God first? Because we've never been this way before! Nobody has! Those whom we might seek counsel from can give us some architectural wisdom, but the creative and procedural flow must come from God directly.

Throughout the Old Testament specifically we see God giving very specific instructions to the Israelites. Battle plans. How to build the Temple. What to eat. God was precise. Why? Because they had never been that way before! They had never crossed the Jordan. They had never faced the giants in the land. They had never taken a walled city like Jericho.

So, if no man on the Earth in all of history has been where we are called to go, that means we have no option to but to actually RELY on uncommon sense! There is no historical data. There have been no books written. It's all brand new. That's why we must be in the prayer room continually! We must be in the Spirit always! God has so much to say to us. The perfect Logos, written Word of God MUST come alive to us! It must be sprinkled with Rhema… God wants to flow through His Word TODAY!

I love to read books. I love to go to conferences. I love to listen to amazing men and women of God teach. I'm nearly addicted to it! I have much to learn and God has done great things through many amazing men and women of God. I honor that and glean as much as I can. But, there is a right way to read books and a wrong way. There is a right way to go to conferences and a wrong way. If we do these things to gain some basic wisdom, to grasp fresh biblical truths, to learn from mistakes and to enhance our personal and ministry lives, then great. But, if we subscribe to someone else's new wine, it immediately becomes old wine to us. We need the Rhema Word of God to speak directly to us.

At Revolution we're currently in the wild pursuit of revival. God is showing up in amazing ways right now. I often joke that when this revival spreads around the world, I just may write a book titled, "Don't Copy Us!" It will be full of blank pages for people to journal their own adventure. What will work for us won't work as a formula for another. Sure, there will be many powerful principles that we'll be able to transfer to others. Many exciting stories. Amazing revelations. But, God has a specific call for us. He'll have a different specific call for everybody else.

I had a vision last night regarding this very topic. I saw this very wide path with thousands of Christians on it. (No, this wasn't the wide path to Hell!) Every person was following another who was following another who was following another. And on and on. This is not what Paul meant when he said, *"Follow me as I follow Christ."* If it was, he would have said something like, *"Follow me as I follow Barnabas as he follows Peter as he follows Fred as he follows Kathy as she follows Lucy as she follows Hank and then, hopefully, if all is well, as Hank follows Christ."*

So, in the vision, as a few of my friends and I were in that flow of people, we heard something from off the path in the woods. *"Pssst! Hey! Over here! It's Jesus! Hey John, you're going the wrong way... come over here!"* In the vision I saw Jesus standing there. He didn't look anything like we'd assume He would. He was a lot like Peter Pan of all people! Youthful, jumping up and down, full of energy, full of life. He was so excited that He got our attention!

"Hey, come this way. Yeah! You can trust me! It's much more fun this way!" Jesus said. I turned to my friends and said, *"Hey, this way!"* I basically said, *"Follow me guys as I follow Christ."*

We all stepped off the path into the woods. We then saw something amazing. Jesus, full of vigor and passion, was running ahead. He kept looking back to make sure we were there. We all ran behind Him, suddenly catching on to Jesus' excitement. We were awe struck as we caught up with Jesus. Jesus had an axe and was chopping down trees and clearing away brush. He was taking us somewhere no man has ever gone. He was making a brand new path for us. Deep inside we all couldn't contain our new found expectancy. We knew that Jesus had something so amazing, so life-changing for us ahead. We wanted to stay right with Him, day and night, as He kept clearing this fresh and exciting path for us. We were truly on an new and earth-shaking mission!

Do we have the courage to leave the path worn out by man? Do we trust Jesus? Will we go even if nobody follows? The answer to that question will determine our destiny.

CHAPTER THIRTEEN

A NEW PRAYERADIGM

"Stop wasting time in prayer."

That's the sentence that burned deep in my spirit. Time is short and the amount of work to be done before Jesus returns is well beyond any human capacity to complete.

But, wasting time in prayer? I've often emphasized the importance of spending hours a day in prayer, in the very presence of God. Was God changing this emphasis? No, He wasn't changing it, but He was refining it. He's not at all drawing His Church out of the prayer rooms. The Holy Spirit is still contending with us to fall in love with simply being with Him in intentional, hungry and lengthy prayer. Our ministry to God in prayer is a primary key in preparing for the coming end-time revival and then the second coming of Jesus. Revelation driven prayer fueled ministries must be established around the world. Deep intercession must be a serious focus for every city. Current churches must allow a pruning of programs and other endeavors to make it possible for every participant to learn the art of prayer every week.

So, what was the Holy Spirit impressing on me when I was told to stop wasting time in prayer?

It's actually quite simple. Let's say a construction company had a deadline to complete a project. The completion of the project was scheduled for one year from today. Hundreds of contractors, a team of architects, supervisors and other people were hired and in place. Now, imagine each person scrambling around without any blueprints or instructions. Based on past experience they presume they need certain items to complete the mission. They talk amongst themselves on how they should begin. Others are still upset about their low pay. Thousands of personal thoughts and hundreds of discussions between teammates as well as contentions between teams are filling the atmosphere. Independent issues are, moment by moment, squelching the voice of the foreman who is holding the day's blueprints and instructions in his hands. The foreman knows that there is a clear goal and that goal is broken down into very obvious and detailed steps. Yet, the workers are consumed with their own issues, needs, wants, frustrations and ideas on how to proceed—while not even knowing what project they are supposed to complete!

The reality is that any foreman would be a fool to hire workers without supplying what they needed to finish the job, or without having the blueprints. They certainly have already received the proper permits, have negotiated with the utility companies, have met with city council and have gone through countless other processes to ensure the project was on target for completion. Now, the workers can relax, listen and work!

We are all workers who must respond with precision to the instructions of our Foreman. To receive His blueprints, we must eliminate distractions–including distractions in prayer–and listen. Our project is earth-shaking, and, yes, there is a quickly approaching deadline. Our missions must be completed at a very specific moment in the near future.

I was once praying with fire and passion alone in the church. I was crying out for any number of needs the ministry had.

"Oh God! Bring in the finances and the people. God, my family needs this and that. God, there is this issue and that issue."

I found myself getting worn out pretty quickly as I was praying. The unction that I often experience was draining out fast. God spoke to my spirit and told me to stop praying. He then said this:

"John, haven't you read in my Word where I have promised to supply all of your needs? If so, why are you asking me to meet your needs? It doesn't make sense. The very fact that you are asking me to meet your needs is a revelation of your doubt. You don't believe me or my Word. You are praying from a position of unbelief. Every word that is birthed in doubt and unbelief and that comes out of your mouth is actually doing more damage than good. Stop praying."

Wow! I wondered how many millions of hours in prayer have been wasted as we have spent time revealing our doubt to God! The Word tells us that it's impossible to please God without faith. I believe doubt is one of the most deadly elements in our lives. A life that is consumed with doubt will lead to a prayer life that sounds more like a whine-fest than a power encounter!

Hmmm. Stop wasting time in prayer. The idea is becoming more intriguing. God wants to introduce a new *prayeradigm* to His Church in these end times.

✓ The key is to only pray according to God's Word. And even further, to pray according to His Rhema Word.

Are you understanding why it is absolutely critical to hear God's voice in order to be successful in life? We must know exactly what God wants so we can come into agreement with it! All of the other issues we leave on the altar.

Most prayer is prayed from the soul which is very aware of human need. It's simply mandatory that we eliminate soul based prayer and discover Spirit driven prayer. This will cause us to move from praying for felt needs to praying for real issues. We won't *pray amiss* as we hear God's voice revealing His heart to us.

What about prayer requests?

I have to admit, I struggle with the concept of prayer requests. Most of the time, when we go around the circle and ask for prayer requests we are diving right into the realm of the soul. Are the needs real? Sure. Do they demand prayer? Usually. Should we stop and pray right then as is directed by the one giving the request? Not necessarily.

Prayer requests reveal information. To pray effectively we need revelation. Let me illustrate:

"Welcome to our small group everybody! I trust your week went well. Let's go around the room and take prayer requests as we begin."

1. Jenny: My mom needs a healing in her body. She's going to the hospital for tests.
2. Bob: I need a promotion at work. More money would remove a lot of stress and enable me to be at church more.
3. Lucy: My friend needs to get saved.

4. Mike: I'm feeling discouraged and would like you to lift me up.

5. Linda: My marriage is going through a struggle right now.

A normal, well meaning yet at least semi-soul based prayer could go something like this:

> *"Lord Jesus we come to you and thank you for your goodness! We pray right now for Jenny's mom. We declare that she is healed in Jesus' name! Be with her and encourage her! And wonderful God we are excited about Bob's promotion! We agree now for favor and open doors! Work a miracle in this situation and set him in a place of great blessing! (Yes, amen, thank you Jesus–heard in the background) And God, we cry out now for Lucy's friend- we call her into the Kingdom now in Jesus' name! We come against discouragement for Mike. The joy of the Lord is his strength! Yes God! And lastly Lord, we thank you for Linda. We pray for a touch in their marriage right now. Be with them in Jesus' name!"*

Sound like a normal prayer request session to you? Sure. Such prayer happens in all types of churches and small-groups every day of the year.

Is it possible that the above prayer had a success rate of less than 50%? Less than 10%? What is the success rate of such prayers in your experience?

The above prayer is based on information, good hearted agreement and felt needs. In that example did you notice any revelation at all?

Let's pray for these fictional people again, except now let's introduce an example of revelation. Prayer like this usually takes significantly more time and a willingness to carry burdens for each other. Each time you see a '…', that represents waiting for God to reveal His heart on the matter. It can take seconds or hours.

"Lord Jesus, we thank you for your amazing love. We want to hear your heart on these issues. We embrace a prophetic atmosphere. Holy Spirit, come as you are and do what you want. We want you alone God!... Jenny, let's pray for your mom. We need to take some time to hear God... is there anything you feel that may be hindering her healing?"

This season could reveal that her mom had unforgiveness in her heart for her ex-husband. The next several minutes would reveal an increase in precision in the prayer as well as a stronger presence of the Holy Spirit. God also reveals the specific demonic entities that are assigned to her mom.

"In Jesus name we command every demonic spirit that is assigned to Jenny's mom to cease activity! You may not obey the orders of your superiors. You must leave in Jesus name! Your strategy has been revealed by the Holy Spirit and it's obvious that God's desire in this moment is for you to go and for a new season of life, freedom, forgiveness and faith to increase in her life! We agree with you Father and declare your heart now to the atmosphere around her mom!"

Do you see the difference? Simply praying for healing would be ineffective because the root issue would not be dealt with.

What if God actually wanted Bob to quit that job? He didn't want him to have a promotion. Do you realize that praying for Bob to be promoted there would actually be praying contrary to God's will? It's a serious matter to say the least!

Lucy's friend needs to get saved, it's true. But what if God gives instructions in prayer for Lucy to call her friend at a specific time, invite her to coffee and see what happens? What if that revelation caused a great encounter to occur that led to her friends breaking down in tears at Starbucks? What if the timing was so perfect that she hit her knees right there and cried out to God—just one hour after writing out a plan to commit suicide? We need revelation, not just information.

What if Mike's discouragement is due to habitual sin, or a generational curse? What about Linda's marriage? What revelation is necessary to pray effectively for her and her husband?

Praying from information alone is often fruitless and can often work contrary to God's will. Revelation is simply mandatory if we are to experience this new *prayeradigm*. Our will must submit to God's will. God's timing must take precedence. Today it may be the right time to pray for breakthrough but not the right time to pray for something else.

Our authority in prayer is incredible when we know God's will in a certain situation. Our authority is weakened when we pray outside of God's will. As is illustrated above, it's rarely possible to know God's precise will in a given situation outside of prophetic revelation.

Some of you might take issue with this, but I encourage you to consider the idea. It's often easy to know God's broad will. He wants to return. He wants people saved. He wants to heal. All of this is biblically true. But what about the process of seeing someone come to salvation? What are God's military precise instructions to see that person come to Christ? What demonic strategies must be dealt with? Is there an angelic visitation that needs to take place? What else does God have in mind?

Allow me to share one more story with you in this chapter. The truth is that God desires that none perish—yet many do. Many people that we pray for end up in Hell. I believe that often we miss praying in agreement with a specific plan of God that He desires to carry out. Praying broadly most often carries little power.

I mailed out 3500 bright red postcards that had one word on the front—PRAY! It was an announcement to the people of Manitou

Springs that we would be holding a special worship and prayer event at City Hall. I received emails from witches who were very upset that we were doing this. As I read one of the emails, God spoke something a bit strange. He said, *"I'm going to get one more senior than her"*.

He didn't give me the instruction to pray hard for the witch who sent this email, but He did prepare me for something great. He needed me to have my focus in the right direction.

I discovered that the witch that emailed me had been practicing witchcraft for 22 years. Yet, God said He was going to *get one more senior than her.*

The night of the event, called "Pray Manitou Springs," we gathered for a pre-service prayer meeting. As we were praying, God spoke something very specific to me, *"Pray that doors are opened for me to visit people tonight."*

That was quite a word! Immediately after God silently spoke that word to me, two people, one right after the other, came up and gave a confirming word. It was dramatically clear–God had some appointments that night. So, I shared the word and we all prayed with laser focus that God would literally visit people in Manitou Springs that night!

The night of prayer continued and then ended. We all went home and went to sleep. The next morning I received a phone call. It was Myrna Bevins, a pastor who was with us the previous night. She said, *"John, it's already started."*

I thought, *"Oh great, what could it be!"* After all, we had received threats and ripples of resistance the weeks leading up to the Pray event. She told me that she received a phone call from a man. She went on to tell me what the man said. *"I had to call a church to tell somebody what happened. I was in my bedroom last night, sound asleep. Suddenly I awakened and I opened my eyes. Jesus was standing by my bed.*

He reached out and touched me, and the moment He did I was consumed with love. I've never felt love like this and I'll never be able to deny God's love again."

I was amazed! Myrna then told me that there was more. She told me that this man revealed that he had been a senior ranking witch for 50 years. Aha! Amazing! *God got one more senior* than the lady who had been a witch for 22 years.

Prayer with revelation, carried out without doubting and with great precision simply works. This is why we know that job one in Manitou Springs is intercession birthed out of revelation. To take a city of this magnitude requires perfect adherence to God's blueprints.

Does this mean we shouldn't pray for someone in need? Of course not. We can always in love lift people up in prayer. We can paint with a broad brush if it is necessary. However, to default to such a prayer method can be greatly limiting. We simply need revelation every day to pray effectively. No more wasting time and energy in prayer. Let's hear God and declare to our atmospheres what He is saying!

CHAPTER FOURTEEN

GUARD AGAINST A WONDERING MIND

Precision. Every one of us desires precision and accuracy in our life of prayer. Throughout this book you've read stories of radical precision in prayer. The amazing truth is that God desires us to pray this way all the time. God once again said something that caught me off guard. *"John, I want you to stop wondering if something is my will or not. It's greatly affecting the precision and effectiveness of your prayer."* This was interesting. I heard this as I was pondering whether or not God wanted something to come to pass in my life. I really thought God wanted this to happen, but I wanted to be a good and humble Christian and leave Him room to not fulfill this desire.

I would often hear my grandmother end her prayers with, *"as you will."* Certainly, this can be an attitude that comes from a humble heart. It is honorable to submit to God that His will is much more important than our will. It is a critical element of answered prayer. We must be entirely submitted to God's will as we put our own on the altar. However, to simply end our petitions with an open ended attitude can cause us to unwittingly come into at least partial agreement with the enemy!

Remember, we have discovered that a life of prayer is not a life of petition. It's a life of hearing God, agreeing with Him and then enforcing His will through declaration, warfare, steps of faith and other action steps. If we are not 100% confident that God wants something to occur in our lives, we become open to a variety of potential endings instead of the single outcome that God desires.

As a result, it can become quite common to accept a strategy of the enemy as an acceptable outcome to a situation! To allow ourselves to wonder even a little bit if God really wants something to happen puts us in a compromised position. The plan of God is greatly at risk since its fulfillment is extremely dependant on our active and focused participation. To ever enter a battle without knowing the precise goal and desired outcome makes little sense. We would be playing right into the enemy's hands. When the enemy approaches us, he would have increased influential power to cause us to submit to his plans. He can be very convincing when we are not honed in on a single acceptable outcome. Here's an example of what I am trying to convey:

I was once thanking God that He made it possible for my wife and I to be debt free. It was a testimony to His miracle working power. I was thinking about several significant miraculous situations that led to our ability to pay off our credit cards and our car loans. I was so excited and thankful to God! I then said, *"God, thank you for causing us to be 100% debt free (except, of course our house loan)."* That phrase in parenthesis was a side thought as I was praying. As I thought it, I became instantly convicted. God spoke directly to me. He wanted us to be 100% debt free and in order for this to happen the house would be included in the payoff. It was a powerful moment, yet I had still another lesson to learn. Over the next weeks and months I would regularly pray about the house being entirely paid off. I had learned many of the lessons that I've discussed in this book, so declaring and warring came quite easy. I enjoyed the pursuit! Then, one day something was revealed. I wasn't actively praying in this moment, but I found my self pondering, *"I wonder if this house is really going to get paid off. Man, that would be great! I really hope I see it come to pass!"*

Aha! There it was! That's when God revealed to me that I had a *wondering mind*. I then recalled several times in the past that during the very moments I was praying about paying off the house, I was leaving room for it not to happen! I was compromised! Did God tell me He wanted to pay off the house loan or not? I had to resolve this issue or I had the potential of coming into agreement with the enemy's plan to keep us in debt.

The fact that I wasn't 100% convinced that God wanted our house paid off was causing problems. I was resorting, in effect, to ending my prayers with *"as you will,"* not as an attitude of submission but as a revelation of doubt. Since the fulfillment of this prophetic word from God was dependent on me and my wife to bust through the demonic strongholds that were keeping it from happening, I had to change my perspective on the situation. I couldn't petition anymore. I could no longer allow my doubt to be covered up with false humility as I would surrender to whatever outcome occurred. Such an attitude resulted in war and faith that were well below what was necessary to see the miracle come to pass. This attitude also caused me to waste time stressing out about God's desire. I was controlled by uncertainty instead of standing in extreme authority and demanding that the situation come into agreement with God's very clear will!

Now, I have so much more time and especially energy as I refuse sadness, despair, frustration and other emotions that are a result of not being 'in control'. A person of authority opens his mouth and causes change. This is what God was leading me toward. After all, if I can't see a house paid off or a sickness dissipate as a result of my active direction, how could I ever demand with fiery authority that an entire city that has been a demonic headquarters for decades become a place of life, healing and freedom in Jesus?

Simply, we must know that we know that God desires something to take place. And, yes, this takes hours of prayer at times! As we know in our spirits, we can stand firm and declare His will and watch miracles happen.

One last surprising side note to this revelation–As I find myself standing firm as an ambassador of my King, when things don't immediately change, it doesn't shake my faith one bit. I simply know that as I do my part that at some point in the future everything, in perfect timing, will come together. A week or month or even years of standing firm without doubting or wondering has not resulted in frustration. Pure energy and excitement continues to explode as I ride the wave of God's perfect plan. In fact, the more confident we are that God wants something, the more powerful and determined our declarations become as time goes by.

It's an exciting way to live to say the least!

So, discover what God wants for you. Dive into the Word of God and resolve as many issues as you can. Listen to His voice regarding a specific desire He has for you. Then, stand firm and enforce His will! If you find yourself wondering if it's really going to come to pass, take your wondering mind captive! Refuse to allow such thoughts to enter in and tell that devil to be silent! Let's hear God and watch His dreams come to pass through our lives of extreme faith, boldness and confidence every day!

CONTACT INFORMATION

John Burton

www.johnburton.net
john@johnburton.net